WASHOE COUNTY LIBRARY

3 1235 02962 1559

S
V

APR 2 1 2005

## DATE DUE

| JAN 09 2006 | | | |
|---|---|---|---|
| | | | |
| | | | |
| | | | |
| | | | |
| | | | |
| | | | |
| | | | |
| | | | |
| | | | |
| | | | |
| | | | |
| | | | |
| | | | |
| | | | |
| | | | |
| | | | |
| GAYLORD | | | PRINTED IN U.S.A. |

D0579692

# Gratins

*To Marielle,*
*a wonderful cook who has created many of*
*the savory recipes in this book.*

# Gratins

## Golden-Crusted Sweet and Savory Dishes

CHRISTOPHE FELDER

Photographs by Jean-Louis Motte
Styling by Lisbeth Kwik
Translation by Linda Dannenberg

Éditions Minerva · Geneva, Switzerland

# CONTENTS

## Sweet Gratins

# Savory Gratins

# Sweet Gratins

# Apricot and Ladyfinger Gratin with Cointreau

SERVES 6

INGREDIENTS:

1 packet (7 grams) unflavored gelatin

11 tablespoons granulated sugar

3 tablespoons Cointreau or other orange-flavored liqueur

18 ladyfinger cookies

4 tablespoons unsalted butter

1 vanilla bean, split in half lengthwise

12 fresh apricots, halved and pitted

2 tablespoons brown sugar

2 large egg yolks

1 tablespoon cornstarch

1/3 cup milk

1/4 cup heavy cream

3 large egg whites

1 cup apricot nectar

3 tablespoons confectioners' sugar

6 small mint sprigs

**1.** In a small bowl, combine the gelatin with 1/2 cup cold water and stir to dissolve. Set aside. In a medium saucepan, combine 1/4 cup water with 4 tablespoons granulated sugar and stir to dissolve the sugar. Bring to a boil over medium-high heat, add 2 tablespoons Cointreau, and stir to blend. Remove from the heat and set aside to cool for 5 minutes. Spread the ladyfingers on a baking sheet or large plate. Using a pastry brush, paint the Cointreau mixture onto the ladyfingers until they are saturated. Use 2 tablespoons butter to grease a 10 1/2-by-10 1/2-inch baking dish. Arrange the ladyfingers in the bottom of the buttered baking dish and set aside.

**2.** Using the tip of a small spoon, scrape out the tiny seeds from inside the vanilla bean and set aside; reserve the pods for another use. In a large skillet, melt the remaining 2 tablespoons butter over medium-high heat. Add the apricots, brown sugar, and vanilla seeds and stir to combine. Raise the heat to high and cook, stirring frequently, for 3 minutes. Remove from the heat and set aside.

**3.** In a large mixing bowl, combine 5 tablespoons of the granulated sugar with the egg yolks and cornstarch and whisk briskly until the mixture is pale yellow. Set aside. In a large saucepan, combine the milk and cream and bring to a boil over medium-high heat. Remove from the heat, then gradually pour into the egg yolk mixture, whisking constantly to blend. Pour the mixture back into the saucepan, return to medium heat, and cook, stirring constantly, until the mixture thickens, about 3 to 4 minutes. Remove from the heat, add the gelatin and the remaining 1 tablespoon Cointreau, and stir to combine. Set aside. Preheat the broiler.

**4.** Make the meringue: In the bowl of an electric mixer, beat the egg whites until foamy. Gradually add the remaining 2 tablespoons granulated sugar and continue beating until the mixture attains an airy, supple, creamy consistency. Using a spatula, gently fold about 1/2 cup of the egg white mixture into the milk and egg yolk mixture, working carefully to maintain the volume; blend thoroughly. Add the remaining egg white mixture to the saucepan, delicately stirring and folding to combine, turning the saucepan as you stir, until the meringue mixture is smooth and satiny.

**5.** In a small saucepan over medium-high heat, cook the apricot nectar until reduced by half. Set aside. Arrange the apricot halves, cut side up, on top of the ladyfingers in the baking dish. Spoon the meringue on top of the apricots, just enough to mound over the center of each piece. Set the pan under the broiler, about 4 inches from the heating element, and cook for 3 to 4 minutes, until the meringue is light golden brown in the center. Remove from the oven and sprinkle the top with the confectioners' sugar. Using a spatula, divide apricots and ladyfingers among 6 dessert plates, drizzle with the apricot nectar, garnish with the mint sprigs, and serve immediately.

# Raspberry-Passion Fruit Gratin in Puff Pastry

SERVES 6

INGREDIENTS:

1/2 pound (1 sheet) purchased puff pastry dough

1 egg, beaten together with a pinch of salt, for glaze

1 package (7 grams) unflavored gelatin

6 ripe passion fruit, pulp scooped out and mashed

1/2 cup plus 2 tablespoons apricot nectar

5 tablespoons orange juice

2/3 cup granulated sugar

4 large egg yolks

2 tablespoons cornstarch

2/3 cup milk

1/2 cup heavy cream

1 tablespoon light rum

6 large egg whites

3 cups raspberries

1/4 cup confectioners' sugar

**1.** On a lightly floured work surface, using a lightly floured rolling pin, roll out the puff pastry to a thickness of 1/8 inch. Using the tip of a small sharp knife, cut the pastry into six 2-by-4-inch rectangles; reserve any extra pastry for another use. Place the pastry rectangles about 2 inches apart on a small baking sheet and, using a pastry brush, lightly paint the top of each with the egg glaze. Refrigerate for 1 hour. Preheat the oven to 350°F. Bake the pastry in the center of the oven for 20 to 25 minutes, until golden brown. Transfer to a wire rack to cool, then carefully split each rectangle in half horizontally. Set aside.

**2.** In a small bowl, combine the gelatin with 1/2 cup water and stir to dissolve. Set aside.

**3.** In a bowl, combine the mashed passion fruit, apricot nectar, and orange juice and beat lightly with a whisk to blend. Add a pinch or two of granulated sugar to taste, if necessary. Set aside.

**4.** In a large mixing bowl, combine 1/3 cup granulated sugar with the egg yolks and cornstarch and whisk briskly until the mixture is pale yellow. Set aside.

**5.** In a large saucepan, combine the milk and cream and bring to a boil over medium-high heat. Remove from the heat. Gradually pour the milk mixture into the egg yolk mixture, whisking constantly to blend. Pour the mixture back into the saucepan, return to medium heat, and cook, stirring constantly, until the mixture thickens, about 3 to 4 minutes. Remove from the heat, add the gelatin and the rum, and stir to combine. Set aside. Preheat the broiler.

**6.** Make the meringue: In the bowl of an electric mixer, beat the egg whites until foamy. Gradually add the remaining 1/3 cup granulated sugar and continue beating until the mixture attains an airy, supple, creamy consistency. Using a spatula, gently fold in about 1/2 cup of the egg white mixture into the milk and egg mixture, working carefully to maintain the volume; blend thoroughly. Add the remaining egg white mixture to the saucepan, delicately stirring and folding to combine, turning the saucepan as you stir, until the meringue is smooth and satiny. Set aside.

**7.** Divide the bottom halves of the pastry rectangles among 6 ovenproof dessert dishes. Spoon about 3 tablespoons of the meringue on top of each pastry half. Spoon 1/2 cup raspberries over each portion of meringue, top each serving with another dollop of the meringue, then dust with the confectioners' sugar. Place the dishes under the broiler for about 3 minutes, until the meringue turns golden brown. Remove from the oven and top each serving with the reserved pastry halves. Drizzle the passion fruit sauce over and around each serving and serve immediately.

# Gratin of Black Cherries with Cherry-Flavored Beer Sabayon

INGREDIENTS:

| | | |
|---|---|---|
| 1/4 cup heavy cream, well-chilled | 2 tablespoons light brown sugar | 2/3 cup cherry-flavored lambic beer, or a fruit-flavored beer, or a light beer |
| 3 tablespoons unsalted butter | 1 tablespoon red currant jelly | |
| 1 1/4 pounds ripe black cherries, stoned; reserve the cherry stones | 6 large egg yolks | 1 tablespoon Kirsch |
| | 1/2 cup granulated sugar | 1/4 cup confectioners' sugar |

**1.** In the chilled bowl of an electric mixer, beat the cream until it forms firm, but not stiff, peaks. Cover with plastic wrap and refrigerate.

**2.** In a medium skillet, melt the butter over medium heat. As soon as it bubbles, add the cherries and the cherry stones, stir to combine, and cook, stirring occasionally, for 5 minutes. Add the brown sugar, jelly, and 2 tablespoons cold water and stir well to combine. Pour into a bowl, remove the cherry stones, and set aside to cool.

**3.** Make the sabayon: Fill the bottom of a double-boiler with about 2 inches of water. Bring to a boil over medium heat. In the top of the double-boiler, combine the egg yolks, granulated sugar, and beer. Whisk briskly for 4 to 5 minutes, until the mixture attains a smooth, creamy, mousse-like consistency. Remove from the heat and continue whisking until the mixture holds soft peaks. Place the pot over a large bowl filled with ice cubes and continue whisking briskly until the mixture is chilled. Add the whipped cream and the Kirsch and gently fold in, maintaining as much volume as possible. Set aside.

**4.** Preheat the broiler. Divide the cherry mixture among 6 ovenproof dessert plates. Spoon the sabayon over the cherries and dust with confectioners' sugar. Set under the broiler for 2 to 3 minutes, until the sabayon is golden brown. Serve immediately.

# Cinnamon-Scented Grape and Raisin Gratin

SERVES 6

INGREDIENTS:

1 stick plus 2 tablespoons (10 tablespoons) unsalted butter, softened

3/4 cup slivered almonds, finely ground to a powder

1/2 cup plus 2 tablespoons granulated sugar

2 large eggs

2 tablespoons heavy cream

1 tablespoon dark rum

1 scant tablespoon ground cinnamon

1 pound seedless green grapes

1 pound seedless red grapes

1/2 cup dried currants

1/4 cup confectioners' sugar

**1.** In the bowl of a food processor or a blender, combine the 8 tablespoons softened butter, powdered almonds, granulated sugar, eggs, and the heavy cream. Blend until the mixture forms a thick puree. Add the rum and the cinnamon and process to blend. The mixture should be thick and unctuous. Set aside.

**2.** Preheat the oven to 425°F. In a large skillet, melt the remaining 2 tablespoons butter over medium heat. When the butter begins to bubble, add the green grapes, red grapes, and the currants. Stir to coat and sauté, occasionally stirring gently, for 3 minutes. Divide the mixture among 6 gratin dishes or 4-inch ramekins. Spoon on the almond cream, using about 3 tablespoons per serving. Dust with the confectioners' sugar, and bake for 10 to 15 minutes, until the topping is nicely browned. Transfer to a wire rack to cool just above room temperature. Serve accompanied by a lemon sorbet if you wish.

**Christophe's suggestion:** This gratin is even more appealing when served with a dish of lemon sorbet on the side.

# Chestnut Cream and Pear Gratin

SERVES 6

INGREDIENTS:

1/4 cup heavy cream

3 large ripe pears, such as Comice

3/4 cup Crème de Marron chestnut cream paste

2 tablespoons unsalted butter

1 tablespoon brown sugar

6 egg yolks

1/3 cup plus 2 tablespoons granulated sugar

2 tablespoons Cognac

1/2 cup chopped candied chestnuts

1/4 cup confectioners' sugar

**1.** In the chilled bowl of an electric mixer, beat the cream until it forms firm, but not stiff, peaks. Cover with plastic wrap and refrigerate.

**2.** Using a paring knife or a small spoon, scoop out the flesh from the pears, leaving about a 1/2-inch-thick border at the edges, so that the pear skin forms a shell. Dice the pear flesh and set aside. Spread the chestnut cream over the inside of the pear shells and set aside. In a small skillet, melt the butter over medium heat. When it begins to bubble, add the diced pear and the brown sugar, stir to combine, then sauté, stirring frequently, for about 3 minutes, until the pear softens slightly. Divide the pear mixture among the 6 pear shells, spreading it over the chestnut cream. Place the pear halves on 6 oven-proof dessert plates and set aside.

**3.** Preheat the oven to 450°F. Place about 2-inches of water in the bottom of a large saucepan and bring to a gentle boil over medium heat. Meanwhile, fill a large mixing bowl with cold water and ice cubes and set aside. In a Pyrex mixing bowl, combine the egg yolks, granulated sugar, and 1/4 cup cold water. Place the bowl over the saucepan and whisk briskly, until the mixture thickens and becomes creamy and pale yellow, about 5 minutes. Remove the bowl from the saucepan and place over the ice water, continuing to whisk until the mixture thickens further and chills. Fold in the reserved whipped cream and the Cognac.

**4.** Spoon the cream mixture over the pears, garnish with the candied chestnuts, dust with confectioners' sugar, and bake for about 10 minutes, until the topping is puffed and browned. Serve immediately.

# Apple, Apricot, and Thyme Gratin with Dark Chocolate Sauce

SERVES 6

INGREDIENTS:

*For the chocolate sauce:*

10 ounces dark chocolate, ideally 70% cocoa content, finely chopped

3 large egg yolks

3 tablespoons granulated sugar

1 cup milk

1 cup heavy cream

*For the gratin:*

1/4 cup heavy cream

1 tablespoon Cointreau, or other orange-flavored liqueur

6 Granny Smith apples

6 ripe apricots

4 tablespoons unsalted butter

2 sprigs thyme

6 tablespoons granulated sugar

6 large egg yolks, beaten

1/4 cup confectioners' sugar

**To make the chocolate sauce:**

**1.** Place the chocolate in a large mixing bowl and set aside. In a medium mixing bowl, combine the egg yolks and the sugar and beat until the mixture is creamy and pale yellow. Set aside. In a saucepan, combine the milk and cream and bring to a gentle boil over medium heat. Reduce the heat to medium-low and gradually pour in the egg mixture, whisking constantly to blend. Cook, stirring constantly, until the mixture thickens and generously coats the back of a wooden spoon, about 5 minutes. Remove from the heat and gradually pour into the reserved chocolate, stirring constantly with a spoon to melt and incorporate the chocolate, until the mixture forms a thick, satin-smooth chocolate sauce. Set aside.

**To make the gratin:**

**1.** In the chilled bowl of an electric mixer, combine the cream and the Cointreau and beat until the mixture can hold firm, but not stiff, peaks. Cover with plastic wrap and refrigerate. Slice the apples in half, core, then, using a sharp paring knife or a melon baller, scoop out the apple flesh, leaving about a 1/4-inch border at the edges so that the apple skin forms a shell. Cut the scooped out apple into bite-sized pieces and set aside. Halve the apricots, remove the pits, then cut each half into 4 quarters. Set aside.

**2.** In a medium skillet, melt the butter over medium heat. When the butter begins to bubble, add the apples and apricots, stir to combine, then cook for 4 to 5 minutes, stirring frequently, until the fruit softens. Add the thyme, stir to combine, then remove from the heat and set aside.

**3.** Preheat oven to 425°F. Fill a large mixing bowl with cold water and ice cubes and set aside. Fill the bottom of a double boiler with about 2 inches of water, and bring to a gentle boil. In the top of the double boiler, combine 1/4 cup water and the sugar and bring to a gentle boil. Pour into the beaten egg yolks, whisking constantly to blend, then return the mixture to the top of the double boiler, cook, whisking constantly, until the mixture turns pale yellow and thickens to the consistency of a light mousse, about 4 minutes. Remove the top of the double boiler from the heat, place over the ice water and whisk about 4 minutes, until the mixture thickens a bit more and cools. Fold in the reserved whipped cream, working carefully to maintain as much volume as possible. Set aside.

**4.** Remove the thyme from the reserved fruit. Fill the apple shells with the fruit mixture and place the shells on a baking sheet. Spoon the cream mixture into the shells, dust with the confectioners' sugar, and bake about 15 minutes, until the topping is nicely browned. Meanwhile, warm the chocolate sauce over low heat.

# Almond, Apricot, and Peanut Gratin

SERVES 6

INGREDIENTS:

1 stick (8 tablespoons) unsalted butter, softened

3/4 cup slivered almonds, finely ground to a powder

1 cup plus 1 tablespoon granulated sugar

2 large eggs

1 tablespoon dark rum

2 rounded tablespoons creamy peanut butter

9 ripe apricots, halved and pitted

1/2 cup sugar-glazed peanuts, candied pralines, or roasted unsalted peanuts, coarsely chopped

1/4 cup confectioners' sugar

1. In the bowl of a food processor, or a blender, combine the butter, almonds, granulated sugar, and the eggs. Process 1 minute, pausing occasionally to scrape down the sides, until the mixture forms a smooth paste. Add the rum and pulse to blend. Add 1 tablespoon of the peanut butter and pulse to blend. Add the remaining 1 tablespoon of peanut butter and beat to incorporate into a smooth paste. Set aside.

2. Preheat the broiler. Arrange the apricots, cut-side up, on a baking sheet. Generously spread each apricot half with the reserved almond cream. Sprinkle with the chopped nuts, dust with the confectioners' sugar, and place under the broiler for 3 to 4 minutes, until the topping is browned and bubbling. Divide the apricots among 6 dessert plates, 3 halves to a plate, and serve immediately.

# Granny Smith Apple and Raisin Gratin with Almond Sabayon and Cider Granité

SERVES 6

INGREDIENTS:

*Begin preparations for this dessert about 3 hours in advance, to allow time for the granité to freeze.*

2 cups apple cider

5 tablespoons corn syrup

6 Granny Smith apples, cored and cut into 10 wedges

Juice of 1/2 lemon

1/2 cup (8 table-spoons) granulated sugar

6 egg yolks

4 tablespoons apple juice

1/2 cup slivered almonds, finely ground to a powder

1/2 cup raisins

1/4 cup confectioners' sugar

**1.** In a bowl, combine the cider and corn syrup and stir well to blend. Refrigerate for about 10 minutes, stir well, then transfer the mixture to 1 or 2 ice-cube trays. Freeze for 3 hours, scraping the mixture with a fork every 45 minutes to an hour to create the crystals that compose the granité.

**2.** Combine the apples and lemon juice in a bowl and toss to coat. Spread the apples in the bottom of a large skillet, pour in just enough cold water to cover, sprinkle with 3 tablespoons granulated sugar, and bring to a boil over high heat. Cover, reduce heat to medium-low, and poach for 4 minutes. Remove from the heat, drain, and set aside.

**3.** Make the sabayon: Fill a large saucepan with 2 inches of water and bring to a gentle boil. Meanwhile, in a Pyrex mixing bowl, combine the eggs, the remaining 5 tablespoons granulated sugar, and the apple juice. Place the bowl over the saucepan and whisk briskly for about 5 minutes, until the mixture becomes creamy, thickened, and pale yellow. Remove from the heat and continue whisking until the mixture can hold firm peaks. Fold in the powdered almonds. Set aside.

**4.** Preheat the broiler. Divide the apples among 6 deep-sided ovenproof dessert plates, or gratin dishes, arranging them decoratively.

**5.** Spoon on the sabayon, garnish with the raisins, and broil for 3 to 4 minutes, until the sabayon is puffy and nicely browned. Meanwhile, fill 6 stemmed glasses or small glass bowls with the cider granité. Dust the gratins with confectioners' sugar and serve immediately, accompanied by the granité.

# Earl Grey Tea-Marinated Prunes with Sabayon Gratin

SERVES 6

*Begin preparations 7 to 8 hours ahead, to allow time for the prunes to marinate and the compote to chill.*

INGREDIENTS:

4 bags Earl Grey tea

2/3 cup granulated sugar

1 orange, quartered

1 lemon, quartered

30 soft, pitted prunes

1/3 cup coarsely chopped hazelnuts

1/3 cup coarsely chopped shelled pistachio nuts

1/3 cup coarsely chopped walnuts

6 large egg yolks

1 tablespoon dark rum

1/4 cup confectioners' sugar

**1.** In a saucepan, bring 2 1/2 cups water to a boil. Remove from the heat, add the tea and the sugar, stir to dissolve, then set aside. Once cool, remove the tea bags and set aside.

**2.** In a large non-reactive saucepan, combine 2 cups tea, the orange and lemon quarters, and the prunes. Bring to a boil over medium heat. Cook 2 minutes, then set aside to marinate for 2 to 3 hours. Remove the oranges and lemons and discard.

**3.** In a saucepan, combine 12 of the prunes with just enough of the marinating liquid to cover. Bring to a gentle boil over medium heat, reduce the heat to low, cover, and cook for about 30 minutes, until the prunes are very tender. Transfer the prune compote to a bowl, cover with plastic wrap, and chill for at least 3 hours.

**4.** Meanwhile, preheat the oven to 400°F. Spread the nuts over a baking sheet and bake for 10 to 15 minutes, until they are nicely browned. Set the sheet aside on a wire rack to cool.

**5.** Make the sabayon: In the bottom of a double boiler, bring about 2 inches of water to a gentle boil. In the top of the double boiler, combine the remaining 1/2 cup tea and the egg yolks. Whisk briskly for 4 to 5 minutes, until the mixture is thick and creamy, the consistency of a light mousse. Remove from the heat and continue whisking, until the mixture can hold firm, but not stiff, peaks. Fold in the rum and set aside.

**6.** Preheat the broiler. Divide the prune compote among 6 ovenproof dessert plates, then sprinkle the grilled nuts over the compote. Drain the remaining prunes and place 3 on each plate, around the prune compote. Spoon the sabayon over the prunes (leaving the compote bare), and in a circle around the edge of the plates. Dust with confectioners' sugar and broil for 3 to 4 minutes, until the sabayon is nicely browned. Serve immediately.

# Sautéed Apricot and Walnut Gratin with Port Sabayon

SERVES 6

INGREDIENTS:

| 1/3 cup heavy cream | 1/4 cup light brown sugar | 1/2 cup tawny port wine |
| 16 apricots | 3/4 cup red currants | 1/4 cup confectioners' sugar |
| 2 tablespoons unsalted butter | 6 large egg yolks | |
| 1/2 cup walnuts, finely chopped | 6 tablespoons granulated sugar | 1/3 cup pistachio nuts, coarsely chopped |

**1.** In the chilled bowl of an electric mixer, beat the cream until it forms firm, but not stiff, peaks. Cover with plastic wrap and refrigerate. Halve and pit 12 of the apricots and set aside. Halve, pit, and thinly slice the remaining 4 apricots, then divide among 6 ovenproof dessert bowls, lining the bottom and sides with the apricot slices. Set aside.

**2.** In a large skillet, melt the butter over medium heat, then add the reserved apricot halves, walnuts, and the brown sugar, and stir to combine. Sauté, stirring gently occasionally, until the apricots soften, about 5 to 7 minutes. Set aside 6 apricot halves; divide the rest among the dessert bowls, placing 3 halves in the bottom of each bowl. Set aside 18 currants for the garnish; scatter the remaining currants among the bowls and set aside.

**3.** Make the sabayon: Fill a large mixing bowl with cold water and ice cubes and set aside. Fill a large saucepan with about 2 inches of water and bring to a gentle boil over medium heat. In a Pyrex mixing bowl, combine the egg yolks, the granulated sugar, and the port. Place the bowl over the boiling water and whisk vigorously until the mixture thickens to the consistency of a light mousse, about 3 to 4 minutes. Remove from the heat and whisk for 1 minute. Place the bowl partially into the ice-water bath and continue whisking until the mixture cools, about 3 to 4 minutes. Add the whipped cream and gently fold in.

**4.** Preheat the broiler. Reserve about 1/2 cup of the sabayon; divide the remaining sabayon among the dessert bowls. In the center of each bowl, place 1 of the reserved apricot halves, cut side up. Fill the indentation in each with a spoonful of the reserved sabayon. Dust with the confectioners' sugar, then place under the broiler for 3 to 4 minutes, until the sabayon is browned and bubbling. Garnish with the reserved currants and the pistachio nuts. Serve immediately.

# Papaya, Pineapple, and Peppered Lemon Gratin with Orange Sabayon

SERVES 6

INGREDIENTS:

1/4 cup heavy cream

3 papayas, at least half yellow and slightly yielding to the touch; peeled, quartered, seeded, and diced

1 ripe pineapple, peeled, cored, halved, then cut into 1/3-inch slices

Juice of 1 lemon

Coarsely ground black pepper

6 large egg yolks

1/2 cup granulated sugar

5 tablespoons fresh orange juice

1 tablespoon light rum

1/4 cup confectioners' sugar

**1.** In the chilled bowl of an electric mixer, beat the cream until it forms firm, but not stiff, peaks. Cover with plastic wrap and refrigerate. In a mixing bowl, combine the papaya, pineapple, and the lemon juice and toss gently to combine. Divide among 6 ovenproof soup bowls or gratin dishes. Sprinkle each serving with a pinch of pepper and set aside.

**2.** Make the sabayon: Fill a large mixing bowl with cold water and ice cubes and set aside. Fill a large saucepan with about 2 inches of water and bring to a gentle boil over medium heat. In a Pyrex mixing bowl, combine the egg yolks, granulated sugar, and orange juice. Place over the boiling water and whisk vigorously until the mixture thickens to the consistency of a light mousse, about 3 to 4 minutes. Remove from the heat and whisk for 1 minute. Place the bowl partially into the ice-water bath and continue whisking until the mixture cools, about 3 to 4 minutes. Add the whipped cream and the rum and gently fold in.

**3.** Preheat the broiler. Divide the sabayon among the fruit servings, spooning it evenly over the top. Dust with the confectioners' sugar, then place under the broiler for 2 to 3 minutes, until the sabayon is browned and bubbling. Serve immediately.

# Vanilla Rhubarb Gratin

SERVES 6

INGREDIENTS:

1 packet (7 grams) unflavored gelatin

3 tablespoons unsalted butter

2 pounds rhubarb, with deep-red stalks, peeled if stringy, cut into 1-inch pieces

3 tablespoons wild-flower or pine honey

3/4 cup plus 2 tablespoons granulated sugar

5 large egg yolks

2 tablespoons cornstarch

2/3 cup milk

1/2 cup heavy cream

2 vanilla beans, split lengthwise

1 tablespoon Kirsch

6 large egg whites

1/4 cup confectioners' sugar

1/3 cup chopped candied lemon or orange peel as garnish (optional)

**1.** In a small bowl, combine the gelatin with 1/2 cup cold water, stir to dissolve and set aside. In a large saucepan, melt the butter over medium heat. Add the rhubarb, honey, and 1/4 cup granulated sugar and stir to combine. Add 1/4 cup water, raise the heat to medium-high and bring to a boil, stirring occasionally. Reduce the heat to low, cover, and simmer, stirring occasionally, until the rhubarb is very tender, about 10 to 12 minutes. Remove from the heat and set aside to cool for at least 1 hour.

**2.** In a mixing bowl, combine the egg yolks, the remaining 5 tablespoons granulated sugar, and the cornstarch. Whisk briskly until the mixture is smoothly blended and pale yellow. Set aside. In a saucepan, combine the milk, cream, and the vanilla beans and bring to a boil over medium heat. Remove immediately from the heat and, whisking constantly, gradually pour into the egg yolk mixture. Return to the saucepan, lower heat to medium-low, and cook, stirring constantly, until the mixture thickens, about 4 minutes. Remove from the heat, remove the vanilla beans, add the gelatin mixture and the Kirsch, and stir to incorporate. Set aside.

**3.** Preheat the broiler. In the bowl of an electric mixer, beat the egg whites until frothy. Add 2 tablespoons granulated sugar and beat until the mixture forms soft peaks. Add the remaining 3 tablespoons granulated sugar and beat until the mixture forms firm, but not stiff, peaks. Add a cup of the meringue to the cream mixture and fold in to incorporate. Add the remaining meringue to the cream mixture and fold in, working carefully to maintain as much volume as possible. Be sure to fold from the bottom of the pan up so that the meringue is evenly incorporated.

**4.** Spoon the meringue mixture over the rhubarb mixture, dust with the confectioners' sugar and broil for 3 to 4 minutes, until the meringue topping is puffed and golden brown. Garnish with the candied lemon or orange peel, if you wish, and serve immediately.

# Semolina and Mirabelle Gratin

SERVES 6

INGREDIENTS:

*This recipe calls for tiny, yellow mirabelle plums. If you cannot find them at your market, substitute 2 pounds of white cherries or golden-gage plums.*

3 tablespoons unsalted butter

2 pounds mirabelle plums, pitted

1/4 cup plus 1/3 cup (9 tablespoons) granulated sugar

Ground allspice or ground cinnamon

1 vanilla bean, split lengthwise, seeds scraped out and reserved; pod reserved for another use

4 cups milk

6 tablespoons semolina

Zest of 1 orange

Fine sea salt

1/4 cup confectioners' sugar

1/4 cup light brown sugar

**1.** In a large skillet, melt 2 tablespoons butter over medium heat. Add the mirabelles, stir to coat, and cook, stirring frequently, for 5 minutes. Add 1/4 cup granulated sugar, a pinch of allspice, and the scraped vanilla bean seeds, stir to combine, and cook, stirring frequently, for 3 minutes. Divide the mixture among 6 ovenproof soup plates, spreading it over the bottom. Set aside.

**2.** Preheat the broiler. In a saucepan, combine the milk and the remaining 1/3 cup (5 tablespoons) granulated sugar. Stir to dissolve the sugar and bring to a boil over medium heat. Slowly sprinkle in the semolina, stirring constantly, and cook, stirring frequently, until the semolina thickens to the consistency of a creamy oatmeal, about 5 minutes. (If the semolina becomes too thick, stir in 2 to 3 tablespoons of milk or cream to thin slightly.) Add the orange zest, a pinch of salt, and the remaining 1 tablespoon butter and stir to blend.

**3.** Spoon the semolina mixture over the mirabelles, spreading it to smoothly cover the fruit. Sprinkle with the confectioners' sugar and place under the broiler for 3 to 4 minutes, until the topping is lightly browned. Sprinkle with the brown sugar and broil for 3 minutes. Serve immediately.

# Bergamot-Apple Gratin with Chocolate Sauce

SERVES 6

INGREDIENTS:

One 3 1/2-ounce bar dark chocolate, ideally 70% cocoa content, coarsely chopped

1/2 cup heavy cream

2 Earl Grey tea bags

1 large egg

3 large egg yolks

3/4 cup plus 2 tablespoons granulated sugar

6 Granny Smith apples, peeled, cored, cut into 6 wedges

4 tablespoons unsalted butter

1/4 cup confectioners' sugar

**1.** Place the chocolate in a mixing bowl and set aside. In a small saucepan, bring the cream just to a boil, remove immediately from the heat, add the tea bags and set aside to steep for 10 minutes. Meanwhile, in the bowl of an electric mixer, combine the egg, egg yolks, and 2 tablespoons granulated sugar and beat until the mixture is creamy and very pale, about 5 to 7 minutes. Set aside. Remove the tea bags from the cream, then reheat the cream until it just boils again. Remove from the heat immediately and gradually pour into the chocolate, stirring constantly to melt and blend the chocolate. Add one-third of the egg mixture into the chocolate mixture and stir to blend. Add the remaining egg mixture and stir to blend well, then set aside.

**2.** Preheat the oven to 350°F. In a large non-stick skillet, spread the granulated sugar evenly over the bottom and melt, without stirring, over medium heat, until the sugar caramelizes to a golden brown. Add the apples and the butter and stir to combine. Cook for 1 to 2 minutes, until the butter is melted and the apples are well coated. Transfer the mixture to a baking dish, cover tightly with aluminum foil, and bake for about 1 hour, until the apples are very tender. Remove from the oven, raise the temperature to 425°F, and transfer the apple mixture to the bowl of a food processor. Process for 1 to 2 minutes or until the mixture forms a smooth puree. Divide the puree among 6 ovenproof dessert bowls. Top with the reserved chocolate cream, spreading it smoothly over the puree. Dust with confectioners' sugar and bake 6 minutes. Serve immediately.

**Christophe's suggestion:** In the restaurant, I flavor this gratin with a couple of drops of essential bergamot oil. At home you can approximate this flavor by using Earl Grey tea, a tea perfumed with bergamot.

# Red Berry Gratin with Pink Champagne Sabayon

SERVES 6

INGREDIENTS:

2 cups strawberries, halved

1 cup fresh currants

1 cup blackberries

2 cups raspberries, halved

3 large egg yolks

3 tablespoons granulated sugar

1/3 cup plus 2 tablespoons pink Champagne

Finely grated zest of 1 orange

1/4 cup confectioners' sugar

**1.** In a mixing bowl, combine the strawberries, currants, blackberries, and raspberries, and stir gently to combine. Set aside.

**2.** Make the sabayon: In the bottom half of a double boiler, bring about 1 cup water to a boil. Reduce the heat to maintain a gentle boil. In the top of the double boiler, combine the egg yolks, granulated sugar, and Champagne. Cook, whisking briskly and constantly, until the mixture is thick and frothy, the consistency of a light mousse. Remove from the heat and continue whisking until firm enough to hold soft peaks. Add the orange zest and whisk to incorporate. Set aside.

**3.** Preheat the broiler. Divide the berries among 6 ovenproof dessert dishes. Mound the berries in the center of the dishes. Spoon the sabayon over the mounded berries. Dust the tops with the confectioners' sugar (putting it into a small, fine sieve and tapping the sieve once or twice over each serving). Place the plates 4 to 6 inches from the heat and broil for 3 to 4 minutes, until golden and bubbly. Serve immediately.

**Christophe's suggestion:** To enhance the Champagne flavor of the dessert, add 3 to 4 tablespoons Champagne to the berries when you combine them in the mixing bowl.

# Gratin of Honeyed Mandarins with Champagne Sabayon

INGREDIENTS:

12 Mandarin oranges or tangerines, peeled, pith and white membranes removed, sectioned, and seeded

2 tablespoons flower-scented honey

1/2 pound rich short-bread cookies, coarse-ly crumbled

3 large egg yolks

1/2 cup granulated sugar

1/2 cup Champagne

1/4 cup confectioners' sugar

**1.** In a mixing bowl, combine the oranges and the honey and stir delicately to coat. Divide the orange sections among 6 ovenproof dessert plates, arranging them over the bottom. Sprinkle the crumbled cookies evenly over the orange sections and set aside.

**2.** Make the Champagne sabayon: Fill the bottom of a double boiler with about 2 inches of water and bring to a gentle boil over medium heat. In the top of the double boiler, combine the egg yolks, granu-lated sugar, and Champagne. Cook, whisking constantly, until the mixture is thick, smooth, and airy, about 4 to 5 minutes. Remove from the heat and continue to whisk for another 3 to 4 minutes, until the mixture holds soft peaks. Set aside.

**3.** Preheat the broiler. Spoon the sabayon over each dessert plate, dust with the confectioners' sugar using a fine sieve, and then place under the broiler for about 2 minutes, until the sabayon is puffy and lightly browned. Serve immediately.

**Christophe's suggestion:** You can also prepare this gratin using blood oranges instead of Mandarins. To make this dessert even more festive, serve it accom-panied by a flute of Champagne.

# Pineapple Gratin à la Piña Colada

SERVES 6

INGREDIENTS:

1/2 pound golden raisins

3 tablespoons dark rum

1 packet (7 grams) unflavored gelatin

1 large pineapple, leaves attached, quartered

2/3 cup granulated sugar

5 large egg yolks

2 tablespoons cornstarch

2/3 cup milk

1/2 cup heavy cream

5 tablespoons shredded sweetened coconut

6 large egg whites

1/4 cup confectioners' sugar

**1.** Fill a medium saucepan half full of cold water and bring to a boil over high heat. Remove from the heat, add the raisins, and set aside for 2 hours to plump. Drain well, place in a bowl with 2 tablespoons rum, and stir to combine. Set aside.

**2.** In a small bowl, combine the gelatin with 1/2 cup cold water and stir to dissolve. Set aside.

**3.** Using a small sharp knife or a melon baller, scoop out the pulp from the center of the pineapple quarters, leaving the skin and about 1/2 inch of the flesh intact along the edges to form a shell. Arrange the pineapple shells on a baking sheet and set aside. Place the pulp in a bowl and crush it well with the back of a fork. Set aside.

**4.** Place 4 teaspoons of the raisins and some of the rum in a small bowl and reserve. Divide the remaining raisins and rum among the 4 pineapple shells, spreading them along the bottom. Spread the crushed pineapple pulp over the raisins, dividing it equally. Set aside. Preheat the broiler.

**5.** In a mixing bowl, combine 1/3 cup granulated sugar with the egg yolks and cornstarch and whisk briskly until the mixture is foamy and pale yellow; set aside.

**6.** In a large saucepan, combine the milk and cream and bring to a boil over medium-high heat. Remove from the heat and gradually pour into the egg yolk mixture, whisking constantly to blend. Pour the mixture back into the saucepan, return to medium heat, and cook, stirring constantly, until the mixture thickens, about 3 to 4 minutes. Remove from the heat, add the gelatin, the remaining 1 tablespoon rum, and the coconut, and stir to combine. Set aside. Preheat the broiler.

**7.** Make the meringue: In the bowl of an electric mixer, beat the egg whites until foamy. Gradually add the remaining 1/3 cup granulated sugar and continue beating until the mixture attains an airy, supple, creamy consistency. Using a spatula, gently fold in about 1/2 cup of the egg white mixture to the milk and egg yolk mixture, working carefully to maintain the volume; blend thoroughly. Add the remaining egg white mixture to the saucepan, delicately stirring and folding to combine, turning the saucepan as you stir, until the meringue is smooth and satiny.

**8.** Spoon the meringue into the pineapple shells, mounding it slightly. Sprinkle with the confectioners' sugar and place under the broiler until the meringue caramelizes to a golden brown. Arrange the pineapples on 4 dessert dishes, garnish each serving with the reserved raisins and rum, and serve immediately.

# Orange, Dark Chocolate, and Litchi Gratin

SERVES 6

INGREDIENTS:

6 large oranges

4 1/2 ounces dark chocolate, ideally 70% cocoa content, coarsely chopped

2/3 cup heavy cream

1 cup freshly squeezed orange juice

2 tablespoons cornstarch

4 teaspoons Cointreau or other orange-flavored liqueur

8 egg whites

1 cup granulated sugar

18 litchis, shelled, seeded, and coarsely chopped

1/4 cup confectioners' sugar

**1.** Cut off the top third of the oranges and just a little slice off the bottom portions so that they sit steady on a plate. Scoop out the pulp from both the top and bottom portions, removing all pith and skin. Chop the pulp coarsely and set aside in a bowl. Set the bottom portions aside. Finely grate the zest from 3 top portions and set aside. Discard the remaining pieces.

**2.** Place the chocolate in a mixing bowl and set aside. In a small saucepan, bring the cream to a boil, then immediately remove from the heat and pour gradually onto the chocolate, whisking constantly to blend. On 2 or 3 sheets of waxed paper, using a palette knife, spread the chocolate in a thin layer. Place in the freezer to harden.

**3.** In a large saucepan, combine the orange juice and the cornstarch and stir to blend. Heat over medium heat, stirring constantly, until the mixture has thickened, about 2 to 3 minutes. Remove from the heat, and add the Cointreau and the orange zest. Stir to combine and set aside.

**4.** In the bowl of an electric mixer, beat the egg whites, slowly adding the granulated sugar, until the whites hold firm, but not stiff, peaks. Add 1 cup of the egg whites to the orange mixture and whisk to blend. Carefully fold in the remaining egg whites to the orange mixture, working to maintain as much volume as possible. Set aside.

**5.** Preheat the oven to 425°F. Divide the hardened chocolate in half. Break half into small shards, and set aside. Place the other half of the chocolate in a small saucepan over low heat, slowly melting the chocolate.

**6.** Divide the orange pulp among the 6 reserved orange shells. Top with the litchis. Sprinkle the chocolate shards over the orange shells. Spoon the egg white mixture into the oranges, mounding it slightly above the rim of the oranges. Dust with confectioners' sugar, then bake in the center of the oven for 8 minutes. Turn on the broiler, place the oranges on the top rack, about 6 inches from the heat, and broil for about 1 minute, until the meringue is lightly browned. Drizzle the melted chocolate over the meringue and serve immediately.

# Banana, Mango, and Currant Gratin

SERVES 6

INGREDIENTS:

1 packet (7 grams) unflavored gelatin

6 bananas, peeled and cut into 1/4-inch slices

3 mangoes, peeled, halved, pitted, and cut into 1/4-inch slices

Juice of 1 lemon

1/2 cup currants

2 tablespoons vanilla sugar or granulated sugar

5 large egg yolks

2/3 cups granulated sugar

2 tablespoons cornstarch

2/3 cup milk

1/2 cup heavy cream

2 tablespoons dark rum

6 large egg whites

1/4 cup confectioners' sugar

**1.** In a small bowl, combine the gelatin with 1/2 cup cold water, stir to dissolve, and set aside. Divide the bananas and mangoes among 6 ovenproof dessert plates, arranging them decoratively, perhaps alternating bananas and mango slices in concentric circles. Sprinkle with the lemon juice. Rinse the currants and drain, leaving a bit of moisture on the berries. Sprinkle with the vanilla sugar, then scatter over the servings of banana-mango mixture. Set aside.

**2.** In a mixing bowl, combine the egg yolks, 1/3 cup granulated sugar, and the cornstarch. Whisk briskly until the mixture is smoothly blended and pale yellow. Set aside. In a saucepan, combine the milk and the cream, and bring to a boil over medium heat. Remove immediately from the heat and, whisking constantly, gradually pour into the egg yolk mixture. Return to the saucepan, lower heat to medium-low, and cook, stirring constantly, until the mixture thickens, about 4 minutes. Remove from the heat, add the gelatin mixture and the rum, and stir to incorporate. Set aside.

**3.** Preheat the broiler. In the bowl of an electric mixer, beat the egg whites until frothy. Add 2 tablespoons granulated sugar and beat until the mixture forms soft peaks. Add the remaining 3 tablespoons granulated sugar, and beat until the mixture forms firm, but not stiff, peaks. Add a cup of the meringue to the cream mixture and fold in to incorporate. Add the remaining meringue to the cream mixture and fold in, working carefully to maintain as much volume as possible. Be sure to fold from the bottom of the pan up so that the meringue is evenly incorporated.

**4.** Spoon the meringue mixture over each serving of fruit, dust with the confectioners' sugar, and broil for 3 to 4 minutes, until the meringue topping is puffed and golden brown. Serve immediately.

# Sour Cherry, Pear, and Pistachio Gratin

SERVES 6

INGREDIENTS:

1 cup sun-dried sour cherries

2 tablespoons Kirsch

2 packets (14 grams) unflavored gelatin

6 Anjou pears, peeled, cored, and cut into eighths

12 prunes

5 large egg yolks

3 tablespoons cornstarch

2/3 cup plus 1 teaspoon granulated sugar

1 tablespoon almond paste

2/3 cup milk

1/2 cup heavy cream

6 large egg whites

1/3 cup shelled pistachio nuts, coarsely chopped

1/4 cup confectioners' sugar

**1.** In a bowl, combine the cherries with 1 cup luke-warm water and 1 tablespoon of the Kirsch. Set aside for 1 hour to soften.

**2.** In a small bowl, combine the gelatin and 1/2 cup cold water, stir to dissolve, and set aside.

**3.** Drain the cherries. Divide the cherries, pears, and prunes among 6 ovenproof dessert plates, arranging them decoratively in the center.

**4.** In a medium mixing bowl, combine the egg yolks, cornstarch, 1/3 cup granulated sugar, and the almond paste. Whisk briskly until the mixture is frothy and pale yellow. Set aside. In a saucepan, combine the milk and the cream and bring to a gentle boil over medium heat. Remove immediately from the heat and gradually pour into the egg yolk mixture, whisking constantly to blend. Pour the mixture back into the saucepan, set over medium-low heat, and cook, whisking constantly, for about 5 minutes, until the mixture is thick and smooth. Remove from the heat, add the gelatin mixture and the Kirsch, and whisk to incorporate. Set aside.

**5.** Preheat the broiler. In the bowl of an electric mixer, beat the egg whites until they are frothy. Add 3 tablespoons granulated sugar and continue beating until the meringue mixture forms soft peaks. Add the remaining granulated sugar and beat until the meringue forms firm, but not stiff, peaks. Add 1 cup of the meringue to the reserved cream mixture and fold in with a spatula. Then add the remaining meringue and gently fold in, working carefully to maintain as much volume as possible, and turning the bowl frequently as you fold, working from the bottom of the bowl up to make sure all parts of the mixture are evenly incorporated.

**6.** Spoon the meringue mixture over the fruit servings, sprinkle with the pistachio nuts, dust with the confectioners' sugar, and broil for 4 to 5 minutes, until the topping is puffy and nicely browned. Serve immediately.

# Pear and Poached-Peach Gratin with Crème de Cassis

SERVES 6

INGREDIENTS:

| | | | |
|---|---|---|---|
| 1/4 cup heavy cream | 2/3 cup plus 4 tablespoons granulated sugar | 4 peaches | 4 rich shortbread cookies, crushed |
| 2 cups red wine | 2 bay leaves | 2 pears, such as Comice or Anjou | 6 large egg yolks |
| 3/4 cup plus 3 tablespoons crème de cassis liqueur | 1 clove | Juice of 1 lemon | 1/4 cup confectioners' sugar |
| | 1/2 orange | 1/2 cup canned blueberries in syrup, drained | |
| | 1/2 lemon | | |

**1.** In the chilled bowl of an electric mixer, beat the cream until it can hold firm, but not stiff, peaks. Cover with plastic wrap and refrigerate.

**2.** In a large saucepan, combine the wine, 3/4 cup crème de cassis, 1/3 cup plus 2 tablespoons granulated sugar, bay leaves, clove, the orange half, and the lemon half, stirring to combine. Bring to a boil over medium-high heat. Add the peaches and poach for 2 minutes. Remove from the heat and set aside to cool.

**3.** Halve the peaches, remove the pits, and cut 2 of the peaches into very thin slices; dice the remaining 2 peaches very small. Set aside. Halve and core the pears, cut 2 of the pears into very thin slices, and dice the remaining 2 pears very small. Sprinkle the sliced and diced pears with the lemon juice to prevent discoloration. Divide the sliced peaches among 6 ovenproof bowls—preferably glass—and arrange them in a pinwheel pattern in the center of each bowl. Divide the sliced pears among the bowls, inserting them under the peaches in a fan pattern. Spoon the diced peaches, pears, and the blueberries into the center of the bowls and top with the crumbled cookies. Set aside.

**4.** Preheat the broiler. Fill a large mixing bowl with cold water and ice cubes and set aside. In a large saucepan bring about 2 inches of water to a gentle boil. In a medium mixing bowl, combine the eggs, the remaining one-third plus 2 tablespoons granulated sugar, and 3 tablespoons of water. Place the bowl over the boiling water and cook, whisking briskly for 4 to 5 minutes, until the mixture is pale yellow and the consistency of a light mousse. Remove from the heat and whisk about 1 minute, then place partially into the ice-water bath and whisk until the mixture cools, about 4 minutes. Fold in the reserved whipped cream and the remaining 3 tablespoons crème de cassis, working carefully to maintain as much volume as possible. Spoon the mixture into the center of the bowls, dust with the confectioners' sugar, and place under the broiler for 2 to 3 minutes, until the topping is browned and bubbling. Serve immediately.

# White Peach and Currant Gratin with Coconut Sorbet

SERVES 6

INGREDIENTS:

12 ripe white peaches

6 egg yolks

6 tablespoons granulated sugar

2 tablespoons Kirsch

1 cup white currants, or small seedless green grapes

1 cup red currants

1/4 cup confectioners' sugar

1 pint coconut sorbet

**1.** Fill a large mixing bowl with cold water and ice cubes and set aside. Bring a large pot of water to a boil, and plunge in the peaches and poach for about 5 minutes. Using a slotted spoon, remove the peaches and plunge into the cold-water bath for 1 minute. Using a sharp paring knife, peel off the skin (set aside if you are planning to make the "chips"), cut the flesh into eighths, and discard the pits. Lay the peaches on a double layer of paper towels and cover with paper towels to absorb excess moisture. Set aside. (If you are going to make the peach skin "chips," do it at this point.)

**2.** In the bottom of a double boiler bring 2 inches of water to a gentle boil. In the top of the double boiler, combine the egg yolks, granulated sugar, and 1/4 cup water. Whisk briskly until the mixture turns pale yellow, about 4 to 5 minutes. Remove from the heat and continue whisking for 2 minutes. Add the Kirsch and whisk for 1 minute, then set aside.

**3.** Preheat the broiler. Arrange the fruit decoratively on 6 ovenproof dessert plates. Spoon the cream sauce over the fruit, dust with confectioners' sugar, and broil 3 to 4 minutes, until the topping is browned and bubbling. Add a scoop of coconut sorbet to each plate, garnish with the peach "chips" if you have them, and serve immediately.

**Christophe's suggestion:** As a garnish, you can transform the peeled peach skin into crisp peach "chips." Preheat the oven to 350°F, spread the pieces of peach skin, cut side up, on a non-stick baking sheet. Sprinkle generously with granulated sugar and bake about 20 minutes, until the skin is browned and crispy. Place a slice into each scoop of sorbet.

# Peach and Almond Cream Gratin with Strawberry-Rosemary Sauce

SERVES 6

INGREDIENTS:

2 1/2 cups (about 14 ounces) ripe strawberries

2/3 cup plus 4 tablespoons granulated sugar

1 sprig rosemary

1 stick (8 tablespoons) unsalted butter, softened

2/3 cup (about 3 ounces) slivered almonds, finely ground

2 large eggs

3/4 cup dark rum

6 large ripe yellow peaches, halved and pitted

1/4 cup pine nuts

1/4 cup confectioners' sugar

**1.** In the bowl of a food processor or a blender, combine the strawberries and 4 tablespoons granulated sugar and process until the mixture forms a smooth puree. Transfer to a bowl, add the rosemary, and set aside for 1 hour to infuse.

**2.** In the bowl of a food processor, combine the butter, almonds, remaining 2/3 cup granulated sugar, the eggs, and rum and process the mixture until it is smooth and creamy. Set aside.

**3.** Preheat the broiler. Using a small spoon, scoop out just a little bit from the center of each peach half to widen the cavity. Arrange the peaches cut side up on a baking sheet. Divide the almond mixture among the peaches, spooning the mixture into the center and over the top of each half. Place under the broiler and cook for 4 to 5 minutes, until the almond mixture caramelizes and turns golden brown. Remove from the oven and place the sheet on a wire rack to cool slightly. Spoon the strawberry sauce over the bottom of 6 dessert plates, then top each plate with 2 peach halves. Garnish with the pine nuts and a fine dusting of confectioners' sugar. Serve immediately.

**Christophe's suggestion:** Add 1 to 2 tablespoons of shredded coconut to the almond cream mixture just before processing to enhance this dessert's tropical appeal.

# Fromage Blanc Gratin with Assorted Red Berries

SERVES 6

INGREDIENTS:

1 1/2 cups fromage blanc, lightly beaten to aerate

6 tablespoons granulated sugar

1/3 cup heavy cream

1 teaspoon vanilla extract

2 large egg yolks

2 tablespoons flour

2 large egg whites

Fine sea salt

1 1/2 cups raspberries

1 1/2 cups straw-berries, halved lengthwise

3/4 cup blackberries

3/4 cup blueberries

3/4 cup red currants

1/4 cup confectioners' sugar

**1.** Preheat the oven to 425°F. In a large mixing bowl, combine the fromage blanc, granulated sugar, cream, vanilla extract, egg yolks, and flour. Beat with a whisk until the mixture is smoothly blended; set aside.

**2.** In the bowl of an electric mixer, combine the egg whites and a pinch of salt, then beat until the mixture has the consistency of a light mousse—thickened, light, and airy, and able to hold soft peaks. Do not beat until stiff. Gradually fold the egg whites into the fromage blanc mixture, working carefully to maintain as much air and loft as possible. The mixture should be smooth and completely blended.

**3.** In a mixing bowl, combine the raspberries, strawberries, blackberries, blueberries, and currants. Place 3/4 cup of the fruit mixture in a small bowl and set aside for garnish. Divide the remaining fruit mixture among 6 ovenproof bowls, using about 1 cup berries per serving. Spoon the fromage blanc mixture over the fruit, then bake in the center of the oven for 20 to 25 minutes, until the fromage blanc topping is puffy and nicely browned. Remove from the oven and sprinkle with half of the confectioners' sugar. Garnish each serving with the reserved berries, placing them in the cracks of the crust. Dust each serving with the remaining confectioners' sugar and serve immediately.

**Christophe's suggestions:** You can prepare this dessert 1 to 2 hours ahead of time, without garnishing with the reserved fruit or the second half of the confectioners' sugar. Set aside but do not refrigerate. Just before serving, preheat the oven to 425°F, then bake the gratins for 5 minutes, garnish with the reserved fruit and final dusting of confectioners' sugar, and serve. If you cannot find all 5 berries, use at least three for a total of about 6 cups of fruit.

# Red and Black Berry Gratin with Lemon-Zest Meringue

SERVES 6

INGREDIENTS:

1 packet (7 grams) unflavored gelatin

9 tablespoons granulated sugar

3 tablespoons cornstarch

5 egg yolks

Zest of 3 small lemons

2/3 cup milk

1/2 cup heavy cream

6 egg whites

2 cups blackberries

4 cups raspberries

1/2 cup blackberry jelly, melted in the microwave or on the stove

1/4 cup confectioners' sugar

**1.** In a small bowl, combine 1/2 cup cold water with the gelatin, stir to dissolve, and set aside.

**2.** In a bowl, combine 4 tablespoons granulated sugar, the cornstarch, and the egg yolks and whisk briskly until the mixture is well blended and pale yellow. Add two-thirds of the lemon zest and stir to combine. Set aside.

**3.** In a heavy-bottom saucepan, combine the milk and cream and bring to a boil. Immediately remove from the heat and gradually pour into the egg mixture, whisking constantly to blend. Return the mixture to the saucepan, place over low heat, and cook, stirring constantly, until the mixture thickens, about 2 minutes. Remove from the heat, add the gelatin mixture, and stir to blend. Set aside.

**4.** Make the meringue: In the bowl of an electric mixer, beat the egg whites until they are thick and frothy. Add 3 tablespoons granulated sugar and beat to very soft peaks. Add the remaining 2 tablespoons granulated sugar and beat until the mixture holds firm, but not stiff, peaks. Place about 1/2 cup of the egg white mixture into the cream mixture and fold in gently. Add the remaining egg white mixture and gently fold in, working carefully—turning the bowl from time to time—to maintain as much volume as possible. Set aside.

**5.** Preheat the broiler. Divide the blackberries and raspberries among 6 ovenproof dessert plates, mounding the berries slightly in the center. Drizzle the blackberry jelly over the berries, then spoon the meringue over the berries. Sprinkle on the remaining lemon zest and dust with the confectioners' sugar. Place under the broiler for 3 to 4 minutes, until the meringue puffs up and is lightly browned. Serve immediately.

# White Peach and Apricot Gratin with Hazelnut Sabayon

SERVES 6

INGREDIENTS:

18 shelled hazelnuts, lightly crushed

6 peaches, preferably white

6 ripe apricots

6 large eggs yolks

1/2 cup granulated sugar

1 teaspoon vanilla sugar, or 1/2 teaspoon vanilla extract

3 tablespoons orange-flower water, or 1/2 teaspoon orange extract plus 2 1/2 tablespoons cold water

1 tablespoon finely ground hazelnuts

1/4 cup confectioners' sugar

**1.** Preheat the broiler. Spread the hazelnuts on a baking sheet and grill for 3 to 4 minutes, until the nuts are well browned. Set aside.

**2.** Fill a large bowl with cold water and several ice cubes; set aside. Bring a large pot of water to a rolling boil, plunge in the peaches and blanch for 3 minutes. Using a slotted spoon, transfer the peaches to the bowl of ice water. Using a paring knife, peel off the skin, cut in eighths, and discard the pits. Repeat with the apricots, cutting each of them in half. Set aside. Preheat the broiler.

**3.** Make the sabayon: In a Pyrex mixing bowl, combine the egg yolks, 5 tablespoons of water, granulated sugar, and the vanilla sugar, set aside. In a large saucepan bring about 2 inches of water to a gentle boil over medium heat. Place the egg mixture over the saucepan, whisking briskly until the mixture thickens, and has the consistency of a light mousse, about 5 minutes. Remove the bowl from the heat and continue whisking constantly until the mixture cools. Add the orange-flower water and the ground hazelnuts and stir to incorporate.

**4.** Spoon the sabayon into 6 small ovenproof dessert bowls. Divide the peaches and apricots (cut side up) among the bowl, arranging them on top of the sabayon. Sprinkle with the grilled hazelnuts, dust with confectioners' sugar, and place under the broiler for 3 to 4 minutes, until the sabayon is nicely browned. Serve immediately.

# Grapefruit and Pear Gratin with Pistachio Sabayon

SERVES 6

INGREDIENTS:

1/4 cup heavy cream

6 large egg yolks

1/3 cup plus 2 tablespoons granulated sugar

2 tablespoons corn syrup

1/3 cup freshly squeezed grapefruit juice

1 tablespoon Kirsch

1/2 cup chopped pistachio nuts

4 pink grapefruit, zest, pith, and skin removed, sectioned

3 large ripe, sweet pears, such as Comice or Bosc, peeled and cored

1/2 cup shredded unsweetened coconut

1/4 cup confectioners' sugar

**1.** In the chilled bowl of an electric mixer, beat the cream until it holds firm but not stiff peaks. Set aside.

**2.** Make the sabayon: Fill the bottom of a double boiler with about 2 inches of water and bring to a boil. In the top of the double boiler, combine the egg yolks, granulated sugar, corn syrup, and grapefruit juice. Whisk briskly for 4 to 5 minutes, until the mixture has the consistency of a light, creamy mousse. Remove from the heat and continue whisking for 1 to 2 minutes more, until the mixture holds soft peaks. Place the saucepan over a bowl of ice cubes and whisk for about 2 minutes, until the mixture cools. Gently fold in the whipped cream, Kirsch, and pistachio nuts. Set aside.

**3.** Preheat the broiler. Line 2 plates with paper towels and place the grapefruit sections on one of the plates for a minute or so to absorb excess moisture. Peel and core the pears, cut them into eighths, and briefly place them on the other plate to absorb excess moisture. Divide the grapefruit and the pears among 6 ovenproof soup plates or dessert bowls, arranging them in an alternating and slightly overlapping pattern. Spoon the sabayon over the fruit, sprinkle with the coconut, and, using a fine sieve, dust the tops with confectioners' sugar. Broil for 3 to 4 minutes, until the sabayon is puffy and nicely browned. Serve immediately.

# Pear Soufflé Gratin with Saffron and Chocolate

INGREDIENTS:

6 ripe pears, such as Comice or Anjou

Juice of 1 lemon

2 tablespoons unsalted butter

2 tablespoons brown sugar

One 7-ounce bar dark chocolate, ideally 70% cocoa content, 1/2 shaved, 1/2 coarsely chopped

4 large egg whites

2/3 cup granulated sugar

Tiny pinch (about 2 threads) saffron

3 large egg yolks, well beaten

1/4 cup confectioners' sugar

**1.** Peel and core the pears, cut them into eighths, and toss lightly with half the lemon juice to prevent discoloration. Set aside.

**2.** In a medium skillet, melt the butter over medium heat. When it begins to bubble, add the pears and the remaining lemon juice and stir to combine. Raise the heat to medium-high and cook, delicately stirring occasionally, for 7 to 8 minutes, until the pears are tender. Add the brown sugar, and cook, delicately stirring frequently, until the mixture caramelizes, about 2 to 3 minutes. Divide the pears among 6 ovenproof dessert plates, immediately sprinkle on the shaved chocolate so that it will slowly melt over the pears, and set aside. Place the coarsely chopped chocolate in a small saucepan and place over very low heat to melt slowly until serving time.

**3.** Preheat the oven to 450°F. In the bowl of an electric mixer, beat the egg whites until they are frothy. Add 1/3 cup granulated sugar and beat until the mixture forms soft peaks. Continue beating, gradually sprinkling in the remaining 1/3 cup granulated sugar, until the mixture forms firm, but not stiff, peaks. Add the saffron and half the egg yolks and fold in; add the remaining egg yolks and fold in, working carefully to maintain as much volume as possible. Spoon the meringue mixture over the reserved pear mixture, dust with confectioners' sugar, and bake for 4 to 5 minutes, until the meringue topping is light-golden brown. Drizzle with the melted chocolate and serve immediately.

# Tropical Fruit Gratin with Malibu Sabayon

SERVES 6

**INGREDIENTS:**

1/3 cup freshly squeezed orange juice

1/3 cup freshly squeezed grapefruit juice

3 ripe papayas, seeded, pulp carved into balls using a melon baller

3 ripe mangoes, pitted, pulp carved into balls using a melon baller

4 kiwi fruit, peeled, halved, and cut into 1/4-inch slices

1 small ripe pineapple, peeled (leaves reserved), halved, cored, and thinly sliced

1/4 cup balsamic vinegar

6 large egg yolks

1/3 cup sugar

2 tablespoons Malibu liqueur

6 mint sprigs

2 tablespoons shredded sweetened coconut, finely ground in food processor (optional)

**1.** In a small saucepan, combine the orange juice and grapefruit juice, bring to a boil, and cook until reduced by half, 1/3 cup. Set aside.

**2.** Arrange the fruit on 6 ovenproof dessert dishes: Alternate papaya and mango balls around the edge of each dish, then fill the center with alternating and slightly overlapping slices of kiwi fruit and pineapple; set aside. In a small saucepan, bring the balsamic vinegar to a boil over high heat and cook until reduced by half, to 2 tablespoons, so that the vinegar has a thick, syrupy consistency. Set aside.

**3.** Make the sabayon: Bring about 2 inches of water to a boil in the bottom of a double boiler. In the top of the double boiler, combine the egg yolks, sugar, and the orange-grapefruit juices and cook, whisking briskly and constantly, until the mixture is smooth, thickened, and creamy, about 3 minutes. Remove from the heat and stir gently for about 1 more minute. Add the Malibu and stir to blend.

**4.** Preheat the broiler. Spoon the sabayon sauce over each serving of fruit. Place the dishes under the broiler and cook for about 3 minutes, until the sabayon sauce is nicely browned. Garnish each serving with a few mint and pineapple leaves, and sprinkle with the coconut, if you wish. Drizzle a few drops of the balsamic vinegar over the fruit and around the edges of the dishes. Serve immediately.

# Chocolate, Mirabelle, and Thyme Gratin

SERVES 6

INGREDIENTS:

*This recipe calls for the tiny, yellow mirabelle plums. If you cannot find these, substitute 2 pounds of white cherries or golden-gage plums.*

1 vanilla bean, split lengthwise

4 tablespoons unsalted butter

2 pounds mirabelle plums, pitted

3/4 cup (12 table-spoons) granulated sugar

2 tablespoons mirabelle eau-de-vie brandy, or Kirsch

1 sprig thyme

4 large egg yolks

2 tablespoons cornstarch

2/3 cup milk

2/3 cup heavy cream

6 large egg whites

One 7-ounce bar dark chocolate, ideally 70% cocoa content, finely grated

1/4 cup brown sugar

1. Using the tip of a small, sharp knife, scrape out the seeds of the vanilla bean and set aside; save the bean pod for another use. In a large skillet, melt the butter over medium heat. When it begins to bubble, add the mirabelles, 3 tablespoons granulated sugar, and the vanilla seeds and, using a wooden spoon, delicately mix to combine. Cook for 4 minutes, stirring frequently, then deglaze the pan with the eau-de-vie and add the thyme, stirring constantly to scrape up any brown bits stuck to the pan. Remove and discard the thyme and divide the plum mixture among 6 ovenproof dessert plates, and set aside.

2. In a mixing bowl, combine the egg yolks, cornstarch, and 2 tablespoons granulated sugar and whisk briskly until the mixture is frothy and pale yellow. Set aside.

3. In a saucepan, combine the milk and the cream and bring to a boil over medium heat. Remove immediately and gradually pour into the egg yolk mixture, whisking constantly to blend. Transfer the mixture back to the saucepan. Place over medium-low heat and cook for 4 to 5 minutes, until the mixture thickens. Remove from the heat, transfer to a large mixing bowl, cover by placing plastic wrap directly on the surface of the mixture, and set aside. Preheat the broiler. In the chilled bowl of an electric mixer, beat the egg whites until they become frothy. Add 3 tablespoons granulated sugar and beat until the mixture forms soft peaks. Gradually add the remaining 4 tablespoons sugar, beating constantly, until the meringue forms firm, but not stiff, peaks.

4. Add 1 cup of the meringue mixture to the reserved cream mixture and fold in with a spatula. Add the chocolate and fold in. Then add the remaining meringue mixture and gently fold in, working carefully to maintain as much volume as possible, and turning the bowl frequently as you fold, working from the bottom of the bowl up to make sure all parts of the mixture are evenly incorporated. Spoon the meringue mixture over the mirabelles, sprinkle with the brown sugar, and broil for 3 to 4 minutes, until the topping is puffed and nicely browned. Serve immediately.

# Fig with Cinnamon and Fresh Almond Gratin

INGREDIENTS:

1/4 cup heavy cream

3/4 cup sugar

3 teaspoons ground cinnamon

18 fresh almonds, or 1/3 cup slivered almonds

1/4 cup milk

6 egg yolks

1 tablespoon raspberry liqueur, or black currant (crème de cassis) liqueur

6 large figs, cut into sixths, or 12 small figs, quartered

3/4 pint (about 1 1/2 cup) raspberries

**1.** In the well-chilled bowl of an electric mixer, beat the cream until it holds firm, but not stiff, peaks. Set aside.

**2.** In a small bowl, combine 1/4 cup sugar with 2 teaspoons cinnamon, stir to blend, and set aside. If you're using fresh almonds, shell the almonds, peel off their skins, and slice in half, then place them in a small bowl with the milk (to prevent them from drying out). Set aside.

**3.** Make the sabayon: Bring about 2 inches of water to a boil in the bottom of a double boiler. In the top of the double boiler, combine the egg yolks and remaining 1/2 cup sugar and whisk briskly for 4 to 5 minutes, until the mixture takes on the airy consistency of a light mousse. Remove from the heat and continue whisking until the sauce thickens, about 2 to 3 minutes. Place the saucepan over a bowl of ice cubes and continue whisking until the mixture has cooled. Using a spatula, gradually fold in the whipped cream and then the raspberry liqueur, working to gently maintain as much volume as possible.

**4.** Preheat the broiler. Divide the figs among 6 ovenproof plates, arranging them in the center of the plates. Sprinkle with 2 tablespoons of the sugar-cinnamon mixture. Spoon the sabayon over the figs, then sprinkle with the remaining sugar-cinnamon mixture. Place under the broiler for about 3 minutes, until the sabayon is puffy and lightly browned. Garnish with the almonds and raspberries and sprinkle the remaining 1 teaspoon cinnamon decoratively around the edges of the plates. Serve immediately.

# Pineapple and Mixed-Cherry with Kirsch Gratin

SERVES 6

INGREDIENTS:

1 large, ripe pineapple, peeled, cored, cut into 1/2-inch slices

24 deep-red, ripe cherries, stoned

18 white cherries, stoned

6 tablespoons Kirsch

1 packet (7 grams) unflavored gelatin

1/2 cup milk

6 tablespoons heavy cream

4 large egg yolks

2 tablespoons cornstarch

2/3 cup plus 1 table-spoon (11 table-spoons) granulated sugar

5 large egg whites

12 mint leaves, finely julienned

1/4 cup confectioners' sugar

1. Place the pineapple slices and the cherries into 2 separate bowls. Add 2 tablespoons Kirsch into each bowl, and stir gently to combine. Set aside. In a small bowl, combine the gelatin with 1/2 cup cold water, stir to dissolve, and set aside.

2. In a medium saucepan, combine the milk and the cream and bring to a gentle boil over medium heat. Meanwhile, in a mixing bowl, combine the egg yolks, cornstarch, 6 tablespoons granulated sugar, and whisk briskly until the mixture is frothy and pale yellow. As soon as the milk mixture comes to a boil, remove from the heat and gradually pour into the egg mixture, whisking constantly to blend. Transfer the mixture back into the saucepan, place over medium-low heat and cook, stirring constantly for about 5 minutes, until the mixture thickens. Remove from the heat, add the remaining 2 tablespoons Kirsch and the gelatin mixture, and stir well to blend. Set aside.

3. In the chilled bowl of an electric mixer, beat the egg whites until they become frothy. Add 2 table-spoons granulated sugar and beat until the mixture forms soft peaks. Add the remaining 3 tablespoons sugar and beat until the whites form firm, but not stiff, peaks. Add 1 cup of the meringue to the reserved cream mixture and fold in with a spatula. Add the remaining meringue mixture and gently fold in, maintaining as much volume as possible. Set aside.

4. Preheat the broiler. Place 1 pineapple slice in the center of each of the 6 ovenproof dessert plates; reserve any excess pineapple for another use. Over each slice of pineapple, arrange a circle of alternating red and white cherries. Sprinkle with the mint leaves then spoon on the meringue mixture. Dust with the confectioners' sugar and set under the broiler for 3 to 4 minutes, until the meringue is puffed and nicely browned. Serve immediately.

# Raspberry Gratin with Cola Sabayon

INGREDIENTS:

| | | |
|---|---|---|
| 1/4 cup heavy cream | 2/3 cup Pepsi or other cola bevereage | 4 tablespoons grenadine |
| 6 egg yolks | 2 pints (about 5 cups) raspberries | 1/4 cup confectioners' sugar |
| 1/3 cup granulated sugar | | |

**1.** In the well-chilled bowl of an electric mixer, beat the cream until it holds firm, but not stiff, peaks. Set aside.

**2.** Make the sabayon: Bring about 2 inches of water to a boil in the bottom of a double boiler. In the top of the double boiler, combine egg yolks, sugar, and cola and whisk briskly for about 4 to 5 minutes, until the mixture attains the airy consistency of a light mousse. Remove from the heat and continue whisking until the sauce thickens. Place the saucepan over a bowl of ice cubes and continue whisking until the sauce thickens. Place the saucepan over a bowl of ice cubes and continue whisking until the mixture has cooled. Using a spatula, gradually fold in the whipped cream, working gently to maintain as much volume as possible.

**3.** Preheat the broiler. Divide the raspberries among 6 ovenproof dessert plates, mounding the fruit slightly in the center of the plates. Drizzle evenly with the grenadine. Spoon the sabayon over the raspberries, then dust with the confectioners' sugar. Place under the broiler for 3 to 4 minutes, until the sabayon is puffy and lightly browned. Serve immediately.

**Christophe's suggestion:** Serve this gratin accompanied by a scoop of rich vanilla ice cream.

# Wild Strawberry and Olive Oil Gratin with Lemon Sabayon

SERVES 6

INGREDIENTS:

| | | |
|---|---|---|
| 1/4 cup heavy cream | 2/3 cup light extra-virgin olive oil | 6 large egg yolks |
| 2 pints (about 4 cups) tiny wild strawberries | 1/4 cup whole fresh mint leaves | 1/2 cup granulated sugar |
| | Juice of 2 large lemons | 1/4 cup confectioners' sugar |

**1.** In the chilled bowl of an electric mixer, beat the cream until it holds firm, but not stiff, peaks. Set aside.

**2.** In a mixing bowl, combine the strawberries with 1/3 cup oil, the mint leaves, and half of the lemon juice and stir carefully with a wooden spoon so as not to damage the delicate berries. Set aside.

**3.** Make the sabayon: Fill the bottom of a double boiler with about 2 inches of water and bring to a boil. In the top of the double boiler, combine the egg yolks, granulated sugar, and 5 tablespoons water. Whisk briskly for 4 to 5 minutes, until the mixture has the consistency of a light, creamy mousse. Remove from the heat and continue stirring for about 1 minute. Place over a bowl of ice cubes and whisk for about 2 minutes, until the mixture cools. Gently fold in the whipped cream and all but 1 tablespoon of the remaining lemon juice. Set aside.

**4.** Preheat the broiler. Divide the strawberry mixture among 6 ovenproof dessert plates, mounding the fruit in the center. Spoon the sabayon over the strawberries. Using a fine sieve, dust the tops with the confectioners' sugar. Broil for 1 to 2 minutes, just enough to lightly brown the sabayon without cooking the berries. Drizzle the remaining oil around the edges of the plates and sprinkle on a few drops of lemon juice. Serve immediately.

# Banana-Orange Gratin with Caramelized Pecans

SERVES 6

INGREDIENTS:

*For the caramelized pecan garnish:*

1/4 cup granulated sugar

1 vanilla bean, split lengthwise

3/4 cup whole pecans

*For the banana-orange gratin:*

1/4 cup heavy cream

3 bananas, sliced into 1/3-inch rounds

4 oranges, zest, pith and skin removed, cut into bite-sized pieces, seeded

6 egg yolks

1/2 cup granulated sugar

6 tablespoons freshly squeezed orange juice

1 tablespoon Cointreau or other orange-flavored liqueur

1/4 cup confectioners' sugar

**To make the caramelized pecan garnish:**
**1.** In a small saucepan, combine 4 tablespoons water and the granulated sugar. Then, using the tip of a small sharp knife, scrape the seeds from the vanilla bean into the sugar-water mixture and bring to a boil. Cook for 30 seconds, reduce the heat to maintain a simmer, add the pecans, and cook, stirring constantly, until the sugar crystallizes and coats the pecans. Continue cooking and stirring until the sugar caramelizes, thickens, and turns golden brown. Remove from the heat and transfer the pecans to a small greased baking sheet or large greased plate. Set aside to cool.

**To make the banana-orange gratin:**
**1.** In the well-chilled bowl of an electric mixer, beat the cream until it holds firm, but not stiff, peaks. Set aside.

**2.** Divide the bananas and the oranges among 6 ovenproof dessert plates, arranging the fruit in 2 layers of assorted overlapping slices. Set aside.

**3.** Make the sabayon: Bring about 2 inches of water to a boil in the bottom of a double boiler. In the top of the double boiler, combine the egg yolks, granulated sugar, and orange juice and whisk briskly about 4 to 5 minutes, until the mixture attains the airy consistency of a light mousse. Remove from the heat and continue whisking until the sauce thickens. Place the saucepan over a bowl of ice cubes and continue whisking until the mixture has cooled. Using a spatula, gradually fold in the whipped cream and the Cointreau, working gently to maintain as much volume as possible.

**4.** Preheat the broiler. Divide the sabayon sauce among the dessert plates, mounding it slightly over the fruit. Using a fine sieve, dust the sabayon with the confectioners' sugar. Place under the broiler for 3 to 4 minutes, until the sabayon is golden brown. Garnish with the pecans and serve immediately.

# Gratin of Wild Strawberries and Creamy Lime Meringue

SERVES 6

INGREDIENTS:

| | | |
|---|---|---|
| 1 packet (7 grams) unflavored gelatin | 2 tablespoons cornstarch | 7 egg whites |
| 1 pound tiny wild strawberries | 5 tablespoons freshly squeezed lime juice | 1/4 cup confectioners' sugar |
| 6 egg yolks | Grated zest of 1 lime | |
| 1/2 cup plus 3 tablespoons granulated sugar | 2/3 cup heavy cream | |

**1.** In a small bowl, combine the gelatin with 1/2 cup cold water and stir to dissolve. Set aside.

**2.** Place the ring molds in the center of 6 ovenproof dessert plates, then divide the wild strawberries evenly within the molds. Set aside.

**3.** In a mixing bowl, combine the egg yolks, 3 tablespoons granulated sugar, and the cornstarch, then whisk briskly until the mixture is smoothly blended and pale yellow in color. Set aside.

**4.** In a medium saucepan, combine the lime juice, lime zest, and cream and bring to a boil over medium-high heat. Remove from the heat and whisk the lime mixture into the egg yolk mixture. Pour into the saucepan, cook on medium-low heat and stir constantly, until the mixture thickens, about 2 to 3 minutes. Remove from the heat, gradually add the gelatin mixture, stirring constantly to blend, then set aside.

**5.** Make the meringue: In the bowl of an electric mixer, beat the egg whites until they are thickened and frothy. Add 1/4 cup granulated sugar and beat to very soft peaks. Add the remaining 1/4 cup granulated sugar, and beat until the mixture forms firm, but not stiff, peaks. Place about 1/3 cup of the egg white mixture into the cream mixture and fold gently in. Add the remaining egg white mixture and gently fold in, working carefully—turning the bowl from time to time—to maintain as much volume as possible.

**6.** Preheat the oven to 425°F. Divide the meringue among 6 ring molds, covering the strawberries with a generous portion of meringue, then smoothing the tops with a long palette knife. Gently lift off the ring molds. Using a fine sieve, dust with the confectioners' sugar. Bake in the center of the oven for about 7 minutes, until the tops are puffy and lightly browned. Serve immediately.

**Christophe's suggestion:** Make these individual gratins using six 4-inch ring molds for a perfectly round, finished presentation. If you don't have ring molds, you can prepare this recipe using 6 individual gratin dishes or shallow bowls. If you wish, serve this gratin accompanied by a scoop of any red berry sorbet.

# Gratin of Honeyed Citrus with Crumbled Meringue

SERVES 6

INGREDIENTS:

1/3 cup freshly squeezed orange juice

1/3 cup freshly squeezed grapefruit juice

6 oranges, peeled, pith and skin removed, sectioned, and seeded; zest of 1 of the oranges finely grated

6 grapefruits, peeled, pith and skin removed, sectioned, and seeded

2 teaspoons vanilla sugar, turbinado, or light brown sugar

3 prepared meringue shells, or 6 vanilla meringue cookies, broken into bite-sized pieces

3 tablespoons aromatic liquid honey, such as pine or wild-flower honey

1/3 cup granulated sugar

6 large egg yolks

2 tablespoons Cointreau, or other orange-flavored liqueur

1/4 cup confectioners' sugar

9 strips candied orange peel

1. In a small saucepan, combine the orange and grapefruit juice and bring to a gentle boil over medium heat. Cook, stirring occasionally, until the mixture is reduced by half. Remove from the heat and set aside.

2. Cover a large plate with paper towels. Trim the orange and grapefruit sections to approximately the same thickness, slicing the grapefruit sections in half, lengthwise, if necessary, then place them on the paper towels, and blot lightly. Sprinkle with the vanilla sugar, then arrange them on 6 ovenproof dessert plates, alternating the fruit in slightly overlapping concentric circles, starting from the outside edge of the plates and working in. Scatter the pieces of meringue, then drizzle the servings with the honey, and set aside.

3. Preheat the broiler. Fill the bottom of a double boiler with about 2 inches of water and bring to a gentle boil. In the top of the double boiler, combine the reserved orange and grapefruit mixture, the granulated sugar, and the egg yolks. Whisk briskly for about 5 minutes, until the mixture attains the consistency of a light, creamy mousse. Remove from the heat and continue whisking another 1 to 2 minutes, until the mixture thickens and can hold firm, but not stiff, peaks. Add the Cointreau and the orange zest and stir to combine. Spoon the sauce gently over each serving, then dust with the confectioners' sugar. Broil for 3 to 4 minutes, until the sauce is lightly browned and bubbling. Garnish each serving with 3 strips of candied orange and serve immediately.

# Summer Fruit Gratin

SERVES 6

INGREDIENTS:

1 packet (7 grams) unflavored gelatin

2 tablespoons raspberry jam

6 rich shortbread cookies, preferably sablés bretons

1 1/2 cups strawberries, halved lengthwise

2/3 cup blackberries

1 1/2 cups raspberries

1 cup red currants

1 cup small, seedless green grapes

1/2 cup plus 1 tablespoon granulated sugar

3 tablespoons cornstarch

5 large egg yolks

7 tablespoons milk

7 tablespoons heavy cream

1/3 cup corn syrup

1 tablespoon Kirsch

6 large egg whites

**1.** In a small bowl, combine the gelatin with 1/2 cup cold water, stir to dissolve, and set aside.

**2.** Spread about 1 teaspoon jam over each of the shortbread cookies, then divide them among 6 ovenproof dessert plates, placing them in the center of the plates. In a mixing bowl, combine the fruit and stir gently to combine well. Divide among the 6 plates, mounding the fruit mixture over the cookies. Set aside.

**3.** In a mixing bowl, combine 4 tablespoons of the sugar, the cornstarch and the egg yolks and whisk briskly until the mixture turns pale yellow and is very smooth. Set aside. In a saucepan, combine the milk and the cream and bring to a boil. Remove immediately from the heat and gradually pour the mixture into the egg mixture and whisk to blend. Add the corn syrup and whisk to blend, then pour the mixture back into the saucepan and cook over low heat, stirring constantly until the mixture thickens, about 5 minutes. Remove from the heat, stir in the gelatin mixture and the Kirsch and set aside.

**4.** Preheat the broiler. In the bowl of an electric mixer, beat the egg whites until they are frothy. Add 3 tablespoons of the sugar and continue beating until the egg whites form soft peaks. Add the remaining 2 tablespoons sugar and beat until the egg whites form firm, but not stiff, peaks. Add about 1/2 cup of the meringue to the reserved egg mixture and, using a spatula, fold in gently to incorporate. Add the remaining meringue and fold in gently, maintaining as much volume as possible, folding from the bottom of the bowl up to the top. Turn the bowl occasionally as you fold. Spoon the meringue mixture evenly over the 6 servings of fruit, the place under the broiler. Cook for 3 or 4 minutes, just until the meringue is nicely browned. Serve immediately.

# Banana, Strawberry, and Rhubarb Gratin

SERVES 6

INGREDIENTS:

1/4 cup heavy cream

1 tablespoon flower-scented honey

1 pound rhubarb, peeled, and cut into 1-inch pieces

1 banana, sliced into 1/2-inch rounds then sprinkled with the juice of 1 lemon to prevent discoloration

2 1/2 cups straw-berries, halved

6 medium egg yolks

1/2 cup granulated sugar

1/2 cup confectioners' sugar

**1.** Chill the bowl of an electric mixer for at least 15 minutes in the freezer (or let it sit for 5 minutes filled with ice cubes). Pour in the cream and beat on medium-high until it holds firm, but not stiff, peaks. Set aside in the refrigerator.

**2.** In a large saucepan, combine 2/3 cups water with the honey and bring to a boil, stirring frequently to blend. Add the rhubarb, reduce the heat to low, cover, and cook, stirring occasionally, until the rhubarb is tender, about 10 minutes. Drain, reserving the liquid, and set aside to cool.

**3.** Divide the rhubarb, bananas, and strawberries among 6 ovenproof dessert bowls, arranging the fruit in alternating slices. Set aside.

**4.** Preheat the broiler. In the bottom half of a double boiler bring about 1 cup water to a boil. Reduce the heat to maintain a gentle boil. In the top of the double boiler, combine the egg yolks, granulated sugar, and 7 tablespoons of the reserved rhubarb liquid; save the rest for another use or discard. Cook, whisking constantly, until the mixture is thick and foamy, with the consistency of a light mousse, about 4 to 5 minutes. Remove from the heat and continue whisking until the mixture is firm enough to hold soft peaks. Place the bowl over a large bowl full of ice cubes and continue to whisk until the mixture cools and can hold firm, but not stiff, peaks. Gently fold in the whipped cream. Divide the mixture among the 6 serving bowls, spooning the mixture over the fruit to cover.

**5.** Dust the tops with the confectioners' sugar and place the bowls under the broiler for about 4 minutes, until the tops are browned and bubbly. Serve immediately.

# Savory Gratins

# Easy Onion Soup Gratin with Toast Croutons and Camembert

INGREDIENTS:

5 tablespoons
unsalted butter

4 large onions,
finely chopped

4 cups chicken stock

2 cups dry white wine,
such as Sauvignon
Blanc

Fine sea salt

Freshly ground
black pepper

4 (1/2-inch) slices
country bread,
left out for several
hours to dry

1 ripe round
Camembert cheese,
about 4 inches in
diameter

3/4 cup Gruyère
cheese

**1.** In a large skillet, melt 3 tablespoons butter over medium heat. Add the onions, stir to coat, and cook, stirring frequently, until the onions have softened and turned translucent, but not brown, about 5 minutes. Add the stock, wine, and salt and pepper to taste. Cook, stirring occasionally, for 20 minutes. Remove the soup from the heat and set aside.

**2.** Preheat the oven to 425°F. Toast the bread slices to medium brown. Meanwhile, trim the crusts from the Camembert, then spread the soft cheese onto the toast slices. With the remaining 2 tablespoons butter, grease the bottom and sides of an ovenproof soup tureen or casserole, then line the bottom of the tureen with the toast slices. Spoon the soup over the bread, then sprinkle the top with the Gruyère. Bake for about 10 minutes, until the top is browned and bubbling. Bring to the table and serve immediately, making sure portion includes a toast slice.

# Spinach Gratin with Raclette Cheese

SERVES 4 to 6

INGREDIENTS:

3 tablespoons extra-virgin olive oil

2 pounds whole fresh spinach, rinsed and dried

3 cloves garlic, finely chopped

3 medium shallots, finely chopped

1/3 cup finely chopped Italian parsley

Fine sea salt

Freshly ground pepper

3/4 cup crème fraîche

2 tablespoons unsalted butter

10 ounces raclette cheese, very thinly sliced

**1.** In a large skillet, heat the oil over medium heat. Add the spinach and sauté, stirring frequently, for 15 minutes. Add the garlic, shallots, parsley, a generous pinch of salt, and several turns of the pepper mill and stir to combine. Add the crème fraîche, stir to incorporate, then remove from the heat and set aside.

**2.** Preheat the oven to 425°F. Butter a 10-inch round or 11-by-7-inch oval baking dish. Spread half the spinach mixture over the bottom of the dish, then top evenly with half the cheese, then repeat this process. Bake in the center of the oven for about 20 minutes, until the top is browned and bubbling. Serve immediately.

# Leek and Tomato Gratin with Basil

SERVES 4 to 6

INGREDIENTS:

Fine sea salt

5 pounds slim leeks, roots and fibrous, dark-green ends trimmed, split lengthwise, thoroughly washed to remove grit, patted dry, and sliced into 3-inch pieces

3 tablespoons extra-virgin olive oil

1 medium onion, chopped

10 tomatoes, peeled (plunged into boiling water for 30 seconds to facilitate peeling), quartered and seeded

3 cloves garlic, mashed

1/3 cup chopped Italian parsley

Freshly ground black pepper

2 tablespoons unsalted butter

1/2 cup whole basil leaves

1 cup shaved Parmesan cheese

**1.** Bring a large pot of salted water to a boil over high heat. Add the leeks and cook for 10 minutes, until just tender when pierced with the tip of a small sharp knife. Drain and set aside.

**2.** In a medium skillet, heat the oil over medium heat. Add the onion and sauté for about 3 minutes, until soft but not browned. Add the tomatoes and stir to combine. Add the garlic, parsley, and salt and pepper to taste, then stir to combine. Cook for 5 to 7 minutes, stirring occasionally with a spatula, until the tomatoes release their liquid and soften, but still retain their shape. Remove from the heat and set aside.

**3.** Preheat the oven to 425°F. Butter a 10-inch round or 11-by-7-inch rectangular baking dish. Arrange the leek and tomato mixture in 8 diagonal rows across the bottom of the pan, the leek pieces slightly overlapping. Scatter on the basil leaves, sprinkle evenly with the cheese, and bake in the center of the oven for about 15 minutes, until the top is browned and bubbling. Serve immediately.

# Potato and Muenster Gratin

SERVES 4 to 6

INGREDIENTS:

Fine sea salt

2 pounds large Yukon Gold potatoes

2 tablespoons extra-virgin olive oil

1/4 pound slab bacon, rind removed, cut into 2-by-1/2-by-1/2-inch strips

2 large eggs

1/2 cup plus 2 table-spoons crème fraîche

2 tablespoons unsalted butter

Freshly ground black pepper

1/2 pound well-chilled Muenster cheese, thinly sliced

2 tablespoons caraway seeds

**1.** Bring a large pot of salted water to a rolling boil, add the potatoes, and cook for 20 to 25 minutes, until not quite done but just tender when pierced with the tip of a small sharp knife. Drain, peel, slice into 1/2-inch rounds, and set aside.

**2.** In a medium skillet, warm the oil over medium-high heat. Add the bacon and sauté for about 5 minutes, stirring frequently, until the bacon is well browned. Transfer to paper towels to drain. Set aside.

**3.** In a small bowl, combine the eggs and crème fraîche, beat to blend, and set aside.

**4.** Preheat the oven to 425°F. In a buttered 10 1/2-inch round or 11-by-7-inch oval baking dish, spread the potatoes over the bottom, season generously with salt and pepper, then scatter on the bacon. Spoon the egg mixture over the bacon and place the cheese slices evenly across the top. Sprinkle with the caraway seeds and bake in the center of the oven for 15 to 20 minutes, until the cheese is melted and browned. Serve immediately.

# Ratatouille Gratin with Bay Leaves

SERVES 4 to 6

INGREDIENTS:

3 tablespoons extra-virgin olive oil

1 medium eggplant, cubed

3 zucchini, cubed

1 red bell pepper, cut into squares

3 cloves garlic, minced

3 tomatoes, cored and cut into small chunks

1 tablespoon tomato paste

1/3 cup chopped Italian parsley

3 basil leaves, thinly julienned

7 dried bay leaves

Fine sea salt

Freshly ground black pepper

3/4 cup unseasoned bread crumbs

3/4 cup grated Parmesan cheese

2 tablespoons unsalted butter

1. In a large casserole or a deep-sided skillet, heat the oil over medium-high heat. Add the eggplant and sauté, stirring frequently, until the eggplant begins to soften, about 7 minutes. Add the zucchini, and the bell pepper and stir to combine. Lower the heat to medium and cook for 5 minutes, stirring frequently. Add the garlic, tomatoes, tomato paste, parsley, basil, 3 of the bay leaves, and salt and pepper to taste. Cook, stirring occasionally, for about 30 minutes, until the mixture is tender and aromatic.

2. Meanwhile, preheat the oven to 425°F. Transfer the ratatouille to a buttered 10-inch round or 11-by-7-inch oval baking dish. Sprinkle with the bread crumbs and the cheese, then scatter with the remaining 2 tablespoons butter. Insert the 4 remaining bay leaves about 1/2-inch into the top of the ratatouille and bake for about 20 minutes, until the top is nicely browned. Remove the bay leaves and serve immediately.

# Chicken Liver and Salsify Gratin

SERVES 4 to 6

INGREDIENTS:

Fine sea salt

2 pounds salsify, peeled and cut into 3-inch lengths

6 tablespoons unsalted butter

3 tablespoons flour

1/2 cup cold milk

1/4 cup crème fraîche, or heavy cream

Freshly ground black pepper

3 tablespoons extra-virgin olive oil

3/4 pound chicken livers, rinsed and patted dry

3 cloves garlic, finely chopped

1/3 cup finely chopped parsley

3 tablespoons cognac

1 cup grated Gruyère cheese

1. Bring a large pot of salted water to a boil, add the salsify, and cook for 15 to 20 minutes, until just tender when pierced with the tip of a small sharp knife. Drain and set aside.

2. In a skillet, melt 4 tablespoons butter over medium heat. Sprinkle in the flour and whisk to blend. Cook for 1 minute, stirring constantly, then add the milk and whisk to blend. Add the crème fraîche and whisk to blend. Season to taste with salt and pepper and cook for another 3 to 4 minutes, until the mixture has thickened. Set aside.

3. Preheat the oven to 425°F. In a skillet, heat the oil over medium-high heat. Add the chicken livers, stir to coat, and cook, stirring frequently, until lightly browned, about 5 minutes. Add the garlic, parsley, and salt and pepper to taste and stir to combine. Cook for 1 minute, then add the cognac, heat, then carefully light with a match and flambé, shaking the pan until the flames subside. Remove from the heat and set aside.

4. In a buttered 10 1/2-inch round or 11-by-7-inch oval baking dish, spread the salsify over the bottom. Top with the chicken livers. Spoon on the cream sauce and then sprinkle with the cheese. Bake in the center of the over for about 20 minutes, until the topping is browned and bubbling. Serve immediately.

# Endive and Prosciutto Gratin

INGREDIENTS:

Fine sea salt

2 pounds (about 6 medium) Belgian endives with as little green at tips as possible, rinsed and patted dry

1 lemon, sliced

3 tablespoons extra-virgin olive oil

2 tablespoons liquid honey

Freshly ground black pepper

2 large eggs

4 tablespoons crème fraîche

1 cup milk

2 tablespoons unsalted butter

1/4 pound thinly sliced prosciutto

1/2 cup freshly grated Parmesan cheese

**1.** Bring a large pot of lightly salted water to a boil. Add the endives, reduce the heat to maintain a simmer, and cook for 9 minutes. Add the lemon slices, cook for 1 minute, then remove from the heat. Discard the lemon slices, drain the endives well, and lightly pat them dry with paper towels. Set aside.

**2.** Preheat the oven to 400°F. In a large skillet, combine the oil and honey, and heat over medium-high heat until just bubbling. Add the endives and stir to coat with the oil-honey mixture. Season with a pinch of salt and several turns of the pepper mill and cook, stirring and turning occasionally, until the endives are lightly browned on all sides. Remove from the heat and set aside.

**3.** In a bowl, combine the eggs, crème fraîche, and milk and beat until well blended; set aside.

**4.** Butter a 10-inch round or 11-by-7-inch oval baking dish. Arrange the endives in a single layer in the baking dish, then cover with slightly overlapping slices of prosciutto. Pour the egg mixture over and around the prosciutto, sprinkle the cheese evenly over the top, and bake in the center of the oven for about 20 minutes, until the top is well browned. Serve immediately.

# Macaroni and Tuna Gratin

INGREDIENTS:

Fine sea salt

1 tablespoon peanut or other vegetable oil

10 ounces (about 3 cups) elbow macaroni

1 (6-ounce) can solid light tuna in oil, drained

3 cloves garlic, minced

1/4 cup finely chopped Italian parsley

2 large eggs

1/3 cup crème fraîche

1/4 cup milk

Freshly ground black pepper

6 tablespoons unsalted butter

1/2 cup freshly grated Parmesan cheese

**1.** Bring a large pot of salted water to a rolling boil, add the oil and the macaroni, and cook for 6 to 10 minutes, until the pasta is tender, but still slightly al dente. Drain, then rinse immediately with cold water to prevent the macaroni from sticking. Set aside.

**2.** Place the tuna in a mixing bowl. Use a fork to break up the meat, then mash it to remove all chunks. Add the garlic and the parsley and stir to combine. Add the eggs, crème fraîche, milk, and salt and pepper to taste; stir well to incorporate.

**3.** Preheat the oven to 400°F. Using 2 tablespoons butter, grease a 10-inch round or 11-by-7-inch oval baking dish. Spread one-third of the tuna mixture over the bottom of the pan, then cover with one-third of the macaroni. Repeat this process twice more with the remaining tuna and macaroni. Chop the remaining 4 tablespoons butter into bits and scatter over the top of the pasta. Sprinkle with the cheese, then bake in the center of the oven for 15 to 20 minutes, until the top is nicely browned. Serve immediately.

# Escargot à la Française Gratin

SERVES 4 to 6

INGREDIENTS:

14 tablespoons (1 3/4 sticks) unsalted butter

1/2 cup minced parsley

3 cloves garlic, minced

2 shallots, finely chopped

Fine sea salt

Freshly ground black pepper

2 (4 1/2-ounce) cans escargots (36 snails), rinsed and thoroughly drained

36 snail shells, rinsed and thoroughly drained

3/4 cup grated Gruyère cheese

**1.** Preheat the broiler. In a large mixing bowl, mash 12 tablespoons butter with back of a fork. Add the parsley, garlic, shallots, and a pinch of salt and pepper and stir well to blend.

**2.** Insert the snails into the shells. Pack the shells with the herb butter, smoothing the top with a palette knife or the back of a small spoon.

**3.** Arrange the escargot shells on 6 ovenproof escargot dishes or individual gratin dishes. Sprinkle with the cheese, and broil for 4 to 5 minutes, until the herb butter is browned and bubbling. Serve immediately.

**Christophe's suggestion:** You can prepare this dish several hours or even a day ahead of time then refrigerating them until you are ready to cook. The herb butter used for the escargot is equally delicious when used to broil large shrimp or sea scallops.

# Gratin of Garden Vegetables

SERVES 4 to 6

INGREDIENTS:

Fine sea salt

3 medium carrots, peeled and cut into 2-by-1/4-inch strips

2 slim leeks, white and pale green parts only, halved lengthwise and cut into 2-inch pieces

1 medium eggplant, quartered and sliced into 1/2-inch pieces

2 medium zucchini, quartered lengthwise and cut into 2-inch strips

3/4 pound green beans, ends trimmed, cut into 2- to 3-inch pieces

4 small turnips, trimmed, halved lengthwise, and thinly sliced

4 cloves garlic, unpeeled

Freshly ground black pepper

6 tablespoons extra-virgin olive oil

2 medium onions, thinly sliced

3 medium tomatoes, blanched for 30 seconds in boiling water, then peeled and sliced into 1/2-inch rounds

Juice of 1/2 lemon

2 small artichokes, two-thirds of the outside leaves snapped off and discarded, thorny tops trimmed, stem trimmed to 1/2 inch

2 tablespoons unsalted butter

3/4 cup plus 2 tablespoons crème fraîche

1/2 cup freshly grated Parmesan cheese

**1.** In separate pots of boiling salted water, blanch the carrots, leeks, eggplant, zucchini, green beans, and turnips for 4 to 5 minutes, until each is crisp and tender. Blanch the garlic cloves along with any one of the vegetables. Drain and season with salt and pepper; set aside in separate bowls.

**2.** In a medium skillet, heat 3 tablespoons oil over medium-high heat. Add the onions, stir to coat with the oil, and cook, stirring occasionally, for 1 minute. Add the tomatoes, stir to combine, season with a pinch of salt and pepper, and cook, stirring occasionally, for 10 minutes. Remove from the heat and set aside.

**3.** Preheat the oven to 400°F. Fill a medium stockpot two-thirds full of water, add a generous pinch of salt and the lemon juice, and bring to a boil. Add the artichokes and cook for about 20 minutes, until they are just tender when pierced with the tip of a small sharp knife. Drain, quarter lengthwise, remove and discard the fuzzy choke, and set aside.

**4.** Butter a decorative 10-inch round or 11-by-7-inch oval baking dish that you will present at the table. Arrange the vegetables attractively any way you wish: for example, place the carrots, green beans, zucchini, eggplant, and turnips around the edges of the dish; place the tomato-onion mixture in the center, and surround with the artichoke quarters. Drizzle with the remaining 3 tablespoons oil, dot evenly with the crème fraîche, then sprinkle with the cheese. Bake in the center of the oven for 25 to 30 minutes, until the top is browned and bubbling. Serve immediately.

# Baby Shell Pasta with Tomato and Egg Gratin

SERVES 4 to 6

INGREDIENTS:

Fine sea salt

1 tablespoon peanut oil or other vegetable oil

1/2 pound (about 3 cups) baby shell pasta

4 large eggs

6 tablespoons unsalted butter

1 medium onion, chopped

4 tomatoes, peeled (plunge into boiling water for 30 seconds to facilitate peeling), seeded, and chopped

1 sugar cube, or 1 teaspoon granulated sugar

Freshly ground black pepper

1 1/2 cups grated Gruyère cheese

**1.** Bring a large pot of salted water to a rolling boil over high heat, add the oil and the pasta, and cook for about 8 minutes, until the pasta is tender but still slightly al dente. Drain, then rinse immediately with cold water to prevent sticking. Set aside.

**2.** Meanwhile, bring a medium pot of water to a boil, lower the eggs gently in, then reduce the heat to maintain a simmer and cook for 9 minutes. Drain and let cool, then peel. Set aside.

**3.** Make the tomato sauce: In a medium skillet, melt 4 tablespoons butter over medium heat. Add the onion and sauté, stirring frequently, for about 3 minutes, until soft but not browned. Add the tomatoes, sugar, and a generous pinch of salt and several turns of the pepper mill and stir to combine. Cook, stirring frequently, for 15 minutes. Remove from the heat, adjust seasoning to taste, and set aside.

**4.** Preheat the oven to 425°F. Grease a 10-inch round or 11-by-7-inch oval baking dish with the remaining 2 tablespoons butter. Spread the pasta over the bottom of the dish. Pour the tomato sauce over the pasta. Slice the eggs into 1/4-inch rounds and arrange evenly over the top of the pasta. Sprinkle with the cheese, and bake in the center of the oven for 15 to 20 minutes, until the top is browned and bubbling. Serve immediately.

# Artichoke and Bacon Gratin

SERVES 4 to 6

INGREDIENTS:

10 fresh or frozen (defrosted) artichoke hearts

Juice of 1 lemon

15 fresh spring onions, or pearl onions, peeled

5 tablespoons unsalted butter

1/2 teaspoon granulated sugar

1 tablespoon extra-virgin olive oil

1/2 pound slab bacon, rind trimmed, cut into 1-by-1/4-by-1/4-inch strips

3 cloves garlic, finely chopped

1/4 cup parsley, finely chopped

1/4 teaspoon fresh thyme

6 tablespoons crème fraîche, or heavy cream

1 large egg yolk

Fine sea salt

Freshly ground pepper

1 cup grated Gruyère cheese

1. In a mixing bowl, combine the artichokes and the lemon juice, toss to coat, and set aside.

2. In a medium saucepan, combine the onions with 1/3 cup water, 3 tablespoons butter, and the sugar and bring to a boil over medium heat. Cook, stirring occasionally, for 20 minutes, until the onions are lightly caramelized and golden. Remove from the heat and set aside.

3. Meanwhile, heat the olive oil over medium heat, add the bacon and sauté, stirring occasionally, until the bacon is lightly browned and crisp, about 6 minutes. Add the garlic, parsley, thyme, and the reserved onions and stir to combine. Raise the heat to medium-high and cook, stirring occasionally for 5 minutes. Set aside.

4. Preheat the oven to 425°F. In a small bowl, combine the crème fraîche and the egg, whisk to blend and set aside. In a buttered 10 1/2-inch round or 11-by-7-inch oval baking dish, spread the artichokes over the bottom. Spoon in the bacon mixture, then pour on the egg mixture evenly over the top. Sprinkle with salt, pepper, and the cheese and bake in the center of the oven for about 20 minutes, until the top is browned and bubbling. Serve immediately.

# Potato Gratin Dauphinois

SERVES 4 to 6

INGREDIENTS:

1 clove garlic, lightly crushed

9 tablespoons (1 stick plus 1 tablespoon) unsalted butter, 2 tablespoons reserved for baking dish, 7 tablespoons chilled and coarsely chopped

2 large eggs

1/3 cup milk

1/4 cup liquid crème fraîche, stirred, or heavy cream

Fine sea salt

Freshly ground black pepper

2 1/2 pounds medium baking potatoes, such as russets, peeled and thinly sliced

1/4 teaspoon freshly grated nutmeg

4 sprigs fresh thyme, coarsely chopped

1. Preheat the oven to 400°F. Rub the garlic clove over the bottom and sides of a 10-inch round or 11-by-7-inch oval baking dish. Butter the bottom and sides with 2 tablespoons butter; set aside.

2. In a mixing bowl, combine the eggs, milk, crème fraîche, and a generous pinch of salt and several turns of the pepper mill. Spread half of the potatoes in the bottom of the baking dish. Pour half the egg mixture over the potatoes. Cover with the remaining potatoes, then pour on the remaining egg mixture. Sprinkle with the nutmeg, then the thyme, and dot evenly with the 7 tablespoons chopped butter. Season the top generously with pepper. Bake in the center of the oven for about 45 minutes, until the top is bubbling and well browned. Serve immediately.

# Pureed Carrot and Bacon Gratin

SERVES 4 to 6

INGREDIENTS:

Fine sea salt

2 pounds carrots, peeled and sliced into 1/2-inch rounds

10 tablespoons or (1 stick plus 2 table-spoons) unsalted butter

1/2 cup milk

Freshly ground black pepper

6 slices bacon

2/3 cup shredded Gruyère cheese

**1.** Bring a large pot of salted water to a rolling bowl, add the carrots, and cook for 10 to 12 minutes, until very tender. Transfer to a food mill and press to a puree, or puree in a food processor. Cut 8 tablespoons of the butter into pieces and add to the puree. When well blended add the milk and salt and pepper to taste and stir well to incorporate.

**2.** Preheat the oven to 425°F. Transfer the carrot puree to a buttered 10 1/2-inch round or 11-by-7-inch oval baking dish. Arrange the bacon slices over the puree and sprinkle with the cheese. Bake in the center of the oven for about 15 minutes, until the cheese topping and bacon slices are nicely browned. Serve immediately.

# Two-Salmon Gratin with Potatoes and Chives

SERVES 4 to 6

INGREDIENTS:

Fine sea salt

2 1/2 pounds Yukon Gold potatoes

1 1/2 cups chicken stock

1/2 medium onion, finely diced

1 sprig fresh thyme

1 bay leaf

3/4 pound fresh salmon fillet

Freshly ground black pepper

2 tablespoons unsalted butter

10 long chives, chopped into 1/4-inch pieces

3/4 pound smoked salmon, thinly sliced

3/4 plus 2 table-spoons crème fraîche

1 cup grated Gruyère cheese

**1.** Bring a large pot of salted water to a boil. Add the potatoes and cook, uncovered, for about 25 minutes, until they are just tender but not soft when pierced with the tip of a small sharp knife. Drain, peel, slice into 1/2-inch rounds, and set aside.

**2.** In a small fish poacher or in a deep skillet, combine the stock, onion, thyme, and bay leaf and bring to a boil. Place the fresh salmon on the poaching rack, or into the poaching broth, season with several turns of the pepper mill, reduce the heat to maintain a simmer, cover, and poach for about 8 minutes, until the salmon is just cooked through. Remove from the heat, transfer the salmon to a plate, and set aside.

**3.** Preheat the oven to 425°F. Butter the bottom and sides of a 10-inch round or 11-by-7-inch oval baking dish. Layer half of the potatoes in the bottom of the pan, then sprinkle with half of the chives. Using a fork, break the poached salmon into bite-sized chunks and layer half over the potatoes, then layer half of the smoked salmon over the poached salmon. Repeat with the remaining potatoes and salmon. Spoon little dollops of crème fraîche over the top, scatter on the remaining chives, sprinkle with the cheese, and season with salt and pepper. Bake in the center of the oven for about 25 minutes, until the top is browned and bubbling. Serve immediately.

# Sea Scallop Gratin

INGREDIENTS:

1 1/2 sticks
(12 tablespoons)
unsalted butter

3 cloves garlic

2 shallots, finely
chopped

1/4 cup parsley, finely
chopped

Fine sea salt

Freshly ground
black pepper

9 scallops

3/4 cup grated
Gruyère cheese

**1.** In a small bowl, mash 10 tablespoons butter with a dinner fork until it flattens and softens slightly. Add the garlic, shallots, parsley, a generous pinch of salt, and several turns of the pepper mill and mix with the fork to combine well. Set aside.

**2.** Preheat the broiler. Divide the scallops among 3 buttered ramekins, 3 scallops per serving. Spread about 1 tablespoon of the butter mixture onto each scallop. Sprinkle with the cheese, then broil for 4 to 5 minutes, until the scallops are cooked through and the cheese is browned and bubbling. Serve immediately

**Christophe's suggestion:** This recipe can be easily doubled to serve 6.

# Gratin of Beef-Marrow Dumplings

SERVES 4 to 6

INGREDIENTS:

*For the dumplings:*

3 marrow bones

3 large eggs

3 cloves garlic, finely chopped

1/3 cup finely chopped parsley

2 medium shallots, minced

Fine sea salt

Freshly ground black pepper

Freshly ground nutmeg

Unseasoned breadcrumbs

2 beef bouillon cubes

2 tablespoons unsalted butter

*For the sauce:*

2 large egg yolks

1/2 cup milk

1/2 cup crème fraîche, or heavy cream

Fine sea salt

Freshly ground black pepper

1 cup grated Gruyère cheese

**To make the dumplings:**

**1.** Scoop the marrrow from the bones and place in a mixing bowl; discard the bones. Mash the marrow with a fork, then add the eggs, garlic, parsley, shallots, and generous pinches of salt, pepper, and nutmeg. Stir well to blend. Begin adding the breadcrumbs a few spoonfuls at a time and mix to blend. Continue adding breadcrumbs until the mixture is firm and not sticky, a consistency that will allow you to form the mixture into dumplings that hold their shape. Mold the mixture into dumplings about 2 inches in diameter; you should have 12 to 16 dumplings. Set aside.

**2.** Bring a large saucepan or casserole of water to a boil, add the bouillon cubes, and stir to dissolve. Using a slotted spoon, lower the dumplings into the boiling broth and cook for 3 minutes. Lift out with a slotted spoon, draining each dumpling well, and place into a buttered 10 1/2-inch round or 11-by-7-inch oval baking dish. Set aside. If your pot is not large enough to hold all the dumplings at once, work in batches.

**To make the sauce:**

**1.** Preheat the oven ton 425°F. In a mixing bowl, beat the egg yolks lightly, then add the milk, crème fraîche, and a pinch of salt and pepper and beat to blend. Pour the sauce evenly over the dumplings to cover. Sprinkle with the Gruyère and bake in the center of the oven for 7 to 10 minutes, until the topping is browned and bubbling. Serve immediately.

# Broccoli Gratin

SERVES 4 to 6

INGREDIENTS:

Fine sea salt

2 pounds broccoli, divided into florets

8 tablespoons (1 stick) unsalted butter

3 tablespoons flour

1 cup milk

1/4 cup crème fraîche, or heavy cream

Freshly ground black pepper

Freshly grated nutmeg

1 cup grated Gruyère cheese

**1.** Bring a large pot of salted water to a rolling boil. Add the broccoli and cook for about 6 minutes, until tender but still slightly crisp when pierced with the tip of a small sharp knife. Reserve 1/2 cup of the cooking liquid, then drain the broccoli and set aside.

**2.** In a deep-sided skillet, melt 6 tablespoons butter over medium heat. Sprinkle in the flour, whisking constantly to blend. Gradually add the milk, whisking constantly, followed by the crème fraîche. Cook for 1 minute, then add the reserved cooking liquid, a generous pinch of salt, several turns of the pepper mill, and a pinch of nutmeg. Stir to blend. Reduce the heat to low and cook, stirring occasionally, for 10 minutes. Adjust the seasoning to taste and remove the sauce from the heat.

**3.** Meanwhile, preheat the oven to 425°F. In a buttered 10 1/2-inch round or 11-by-7-inch oval baking dish, spread the broccoli over the bottom. Spoon the sauce over the broccoli, sprinkle on the cheese, and bake in the center of the oven for 20 to 25 minutes, until the topping is nicely browned. Serve immediately.

## Fennel Gratin with Goat Cheese Rounds

SERVES 4 to 6

INGREDIENTS:

Fine sea salt

Freshly ground black pepper

6 small fennel bulbs, tops trimmed to 2 inches, halved

1 large egg yolk

1/2 cup crème fraîche

2 tablespoons unsalted butter

1 (6-ounce) fresh chèvre goat cheese log, sliced into 6 rounds

2 tablespoons extra-virgin olive oil

**1.** Bring a stockpot of water to a boil, then add 1 teaspoon salt, 4 or 5 turns of the pepper mill, and the fennel. Reduce the heat to maintain a gentle boil and cook for about 20 minutes, until the fennel is just tender when pierced with the tip of a small sharp knife. Drain and set aside.

**2.** In a small mixing bowl, combine the egg yolk and crème fraîche. Add a pinch of salt and a pinch of pepper and whisk until blended. Set aside.

**3.** Preheat the oven to 425°F. With 2 tablespoons butter, grease a 10 1/2-inch round or 11- by-7-inch oval baking dish. Arrange the fennel in the bottom of the dish. Place the cheese slices evenly over the top. Spoon the egg mixture over the fennel and cheese, then drizzle the oil over the cheese. Season with salt to taste, then coarsley grind 3 or 4 turns of pepper over the top. Bake for about 20 minutes, until the cheese and the tips of the fennel are browned. Serve immediately.

# Saffron-Spiced Shellfish Gratin

SERVES 4 to 6

INGREDIENTS:

3/4 cup long grain rice

Fine sea salt

6 large sea scallops

2 pounds mussels, scrubbed

8 prawns or crayfish

1/2 pound medium shrimp, shelled and deveined

4 shallots, halved lengthwise

3/4 cup plus 2 table-spoons dry white wine

1 sprig thyme

3 bay leaves

Freshly ground black pepper

1 stick (8 table-spoons) unsalted butter

1/3 cup flour

3 threads (1 gram) saffron

3/4 cup crème fraîche

1 cup grated Gruyère cheese

1. In a medium saucepan, combine the rice with 1 1/2 cups water and 1/2 teaspoon of salt, and bring to a boil. Cover, reduce the heat to low, and cook 16 minutes. Remove from the heat, stir, cover again, and set aside.

2. In a large casserole dish, combine the scallops, mussels, prawns, shrimp, shallots, wine, thyme, bay leaves, a generous pinch of salt, several turns of the pepper mill, and enough cold water just to cover. Bring to a boil over high heat, then reduce to a simmer and cook for 5 to 6 minutes, until the mussels open and the shrimp and prawns turn rosy. Remove from the heat, discard any unopened mussels, reserve 1 cup of the cooking broth, then drain, and set aside.

3. Preheat the oven to 450°F. In a medium saucepan, melt 6 tablespoons butter over medium heat. When it begins to bubble sprinkle in the flour, whisking constantly to blend. Cook about 1 minute, whisking constantly, then add the reserved broth, and whisk constantly until the mixture is blended and thickened, about 2 minutes. Add the saffron and the crème fraîche, and whisk to incorporate. Season to taste, then set aside.

4. In a buttered 10 1/2-inch round or an 11-by-7-inch oval baking dish, spread the rice evenly over the bottom. Arrange the shellfish over the rice, then top evenly with the saffron sauce. Sprinkle with the cheese and bake in the center of the oven for 20 to 30 minutes, until the topping is browned and bubbling. Serve immediately.

# Baked Seafood Gratin

SERVES 6

INGREDIENTS:

2 pounds well-scrubbed mussels, debearded just before cooking

10 tablespoons (1 stick plus 2 tablespoons) unsalted butter

4 tablespoons all-purpose flour

2 cups milk

4 tablespoons crème fraîche

10 ounces medium shrimp, shelled and deveined

6 large white mushroom caps, thinly sliced

Freshly grated nutmeg

6 large sea scallops

1 1/3 cups grated Gruyère cheese

**1.** In a large casserole, combine the mussels with 2 cups water. Bring to a boil, cover, and steam for about 8 minutes, until the mussels open. Using a slotted spoon, transfer the mussels to a bowl to cool. Discard any unopened mussels. When cool enough to handle, remove the mussels from their shells, place in a bowl, and set aside.

**2.** In a deep-sided skillet or medium casserole, melt 8 tablespoons butter over medium heat. Sprinkle in the flour and stir with a wooden spoon to blend. Slowly add the milk little by little, whisking constantly to blend, then add the crème fraîche and whisk to blend. Add the mussels, shrimp, mushrooms, and a pinch of nutmeg, and stir to combine. Remove from the heat and set aside.

**3.** Preheat the oven to 425°F. With the remaining 2 tablespoons butter, grease 6 scallop shells or gratin dishes. Place a scallop in the center of each shell. Divide the seafood mixture among the 6 shells, spooning it over the scallops. Sprinkle the cheese over the tops, place on a baking sheet or in a large baking dish, and bake for about 20 minutes, until the tops are browned and bubbling. Serve immediately

**Christophe's suggestion:** Serve this gratin in individual scallop shells. You may also use individual gratin dishes.

# Stuffed Zucchini Gratin

INGREDIENTS:

6 medium zucchini

1/2 pound chopped sirloin

1 large egg

1/4 cup milk

1/4 cup unseasoned bread crumbs

Fine sea salt

Freshly ground black pepper

1 tablespoon extra-virgin olive oil

1 medium onion, thinly sliced

3 cloves garlic, finely grated

1/4 cup finely chopped parsley

1 cup grated Parmesan cheese

**1.** Lay the zucchini on their sides. Slice off the top third horizontally, and set aside. Using a teaspoon, hollow out the pulp from the bottom portions of the zucchini, leaving a shell with sides about 1/2 inch thick. Set the pulp and the zucchini shells aside.

**2.** In a mixing bowl, combine the sirloin, egg, milk, bread crumbs, and generous pinches of salt and pepper and stir to combine. Set aside.

**3.** In a medium skillet, heat the oil over medium heat, add the zucchini pulp, onion, garlic, and parsley and stir to combine. Sauté, stirring occasionally, until the onion and zucchini pulp soften but do not brown, about 5 minutes.

**4.** Preheat the oven to 425°F. Add the zucchini mixture to the sirloin mixture and stir well to combine. Stuff the zucchini shells with this mixture, mounding the stuffing slightly above the surface. Cover the stuffing with the tops of the zucchini. Arrange the zucchini in an 11-by-7-inch oval or rectangular baking dish. Sprinkle with the cheese and bake in the center of the oven for 30 to 40 minutes, until the cheese and stuffing are nicely browned. Serve immediately.

# Cucumber and Pancetta Gratin

SERVES 4 to 6

INGREDIENTS:

Fine sea salt

2 medium seedless cucumbers, peeled and cubed

2 medium russet potatoes, peeled and cubed

5 tablespoons unsalted butter

1 cup grated Gruyère cheese

3/4 cup grated Parmesan cheese

3 large eggs

1/4 cup milk

Finely ground black pepper

Freshly grated nutmeg

1/4 cup unseasoned bread crumbs

3 ounces pancetta, thinly sliced

**1.** Bring a large pot of salted water to a rolling boil. Add the cucumbers and the potatoes and cook for 15 minutes. Drain and set aside.

**2.** Preheat the oven to 425°F. Coat a 10 1/2-inch round or 11-by-7-inch oval baking dish with 2 tablespoons butter, then spread the cucumber mixture over the bottom. In a bowl, combine the cheeses and stir to blend. Sprinkle half of the cheese mixture over the cucumber mixture and set aside.

**3.** In a large bowl, beat the eggs, then add the milk and a pinch of salt, pepper, and nutmeg, and beat to blend. Add the remaining cheese mixture and stir to incorporate. Pour the egg mixture over the cucumber mixture. Chop the remaining 3 tablespoons butter into bits and scatter on the top, then sprinkle with the bread crumbs. Cover with the pancetta slices and bake in the center of the oven for 20 to 25 minutes, until the pancetta is crisp and nicely browned. Serve immediately.

# Cauliflower and St. Marcellin Cheese Gratin

SERVES 4 to 6

INGREDIENTS:

7 tablespoons unsalted butter

2 medium onions, thinly sliced

1/4 pound slab bacon, rind removed, cut into 1-by-1/4-by-1/4-inch strips

Freshly ground black pepper

Fine sea salt

1 medium head cauliflower (1 1/2 to 2 pounds), divided into florets

2 St. Marcellin cheeses, or 1/4 pound fontina, thinly sliced

1/2 teaspoon fresh thyme

3 bay leaves

**1.** In a skillet, heat 2 tablespoons butter over medium heat. Add the onions and the bacon, stir to coat, and cook, stirring frequently, until the onions are soft and golden and the bacon has browned, about 10 minutes. Season with pepper and set aside.

**2.** Bring a large pot of salted water to a boil, add the cauliflower, and cook for 6 to 8 minutes, until just tender. Drain, then combine the cauliflower with 3 tablespoons butter and toss gently to coat. Set aside.

**3.** Preheat the oven to 425°F. In a buttered 10 1/2-inch round or 11-by-7-inch oval baking dish, arrange the cauliflower to cover the bottom. Spoon on the onion mixture, then cover the top with the cheese slices. Sprinkle with the thyme and garnish with the bay leaves, then bake in the center of the oven for about 20 minutes, until the cheese topping is browned and bubbling. Serve immediately.

**Christophe's suggestion:** This recipe calls for the luscious, soft and creamy cow's-milk cheese St. Marcellin, from the Alpine Isère region of France. An acceptable substitute, if you can't find St. Marcellin, would be a fontina cheese.

# Tagliatelle and Mushroom Gratin

SERVES 4 to 6

INGREDIENTS:

1/2 pound white or chanterelle mushrooms, trimmed to 1 inch from caps

Juice of 1 lemon

Fine sea salt

2 tablespoons peanut oil

1 pound tagliatelle pasta

3 tablespoons extra-virgin olive oil

Freshly ground black pepper

3 cloves garlic, finely chopped

1/3 cup finely chopped parsley

1 large egg yolk

1/2 cup crème fraîche, or heavy cream

1 cup grated Gruyère cheese

**1.** Cut the mushrooms into 1/4-inch slices. In a small mixing bowl, combine the mushrooms with the lemon juice, toss to coat, and set aside.

**2.** Bring a large pot of salted water to a rolling boil, add the peanut oil and the pasta, and cook for 8 to 10 minutes, until tender. Drain and set aside.

**3.** In a skillet, heat the oil over medium-high heat. Add the mushrooms, stir to coat, then add a generous pinch of salt, several turns of the pepper mill, the garlic, and parsley and stir to combine. Sauté, stirring frequently, until the mushrooms are lightly browned, about 6 to 8 minutes. Set aside.

**4.** Meanwhile, preheat the broiler. In a small bowl, combine the egg yolk, crème fraîche, and a pinch of salt and pepper and whisk to blend. Set aside. In a large bowl, combine the pasta and the mushroom mixture and toss lightly to combine. Add the egg mixture to the pasta and toss lightly to mix. Transfer the pasta mixture to a buttered 10 1/2-inch round or 11-by-7-inch oval baking dish. Sprinkle the cheese over the top of the dish and broil for 4 to 5 minutes, until browned and bubbling. Serve immediately.

# Haddock and Tomato Gratin

SERVES 4 to 6

INGREDIENTS:

1 medium onion, chopped

1 carrot, chopped

1 bouquet garni (1 sprig thyme, 1 sprig parsley, and 1 bay leaf tied in a small cheese-cloth sack)

1/2 cup white wine

3 tablespoons white wine vinegar

Fine sea salt

Freshly ground black pepper

2 pounds haddock or cod fillets (1 large or 2 medium fillets)

10 tablespoons (1 stick plus 2 table-spoons) unsalted butter

2 tablespoons flour

2 cups milk

1 1/2 cups grated Gruyère cheese

1/3 cup chopped parsley

Freshly grated nutmeg

7 tablespoons crème fraîche

3 medium tomatoes, peeled, (plunged into boiling water for 30 seconds to facilitate peeling), and sliced into 1/4-inch rounds

**1.** In a large saucepan, combine 4 cups water with the onion, carrot, bouquet garni, wine, vinegar, and a pinch of salt and pepper and bring to a boil over high heat. Add the fish and reduce the heat to maintain a simmer, and poach for about 10 minutes, until the fish is just tender. Meanwhile, coat a 10 1/2-inch round or 11-by-7-inch oval baking dish with 2 tablespoons butter, then, using a slotted spatula, transfer the fish to the dish and set aside. Reserve the poaching liquid (which is a variation of a court bouillon), for use as a soup base or another use.

**2.** Preheat the oven to 425°F. In a small skillet, heat 6 tablespoons butter over medium heat. Sprinkle in the flour, whisking constantly to blend. Cook for 1 minute, then slowly add the milk, whisking constantly to blend. Cook for 2 to 3 minutes, until thickened, then add 3/4 cup cheese, the parsley, a pinch of nutmeg, the crème fraîche, and a generous pinch of salt and pepper. Stir to blend, then remove from the heat.

**3.** Generously spoon the sauce over the fish. Arrange the tomato slices over the top of the fish to cover, then sprinkle with the remaining 3/4 cup cheese. Cut the remaining 2 tablespoons butter into little bits and scatter over the top. Bake in the center of the oven for about 20 minutes, until the top is browned and bubbling. Serve immediately.

# Salt Cod Gratin Provençal

SERVES 4 to 6

INGREDIENTS:

1 3/4 pounds salt cod in 3 or 4 pieces

1/2 pound tiny new potatoes

7 tablespoons extra-virgin olive oil

Freshly ground black pepper

1 red bell pepper, cored and cut into 1/2-inch rings

1 green bell pepper, cored and cut into 1/2-inch rings

1 medium onion, chopped

2 medium tomatoes, peeled (plunged into boiling water for 30 seconds to facilitate peeling), quartered, and seeded

3 cloves garlic, finely chopped

1/3 cup finely chopped Italian parsley

1/2 cup Picholine or other small green olives

1/2 cup oil-cured black olives

Fine sea salt

1/2 cup freshly grated Parmesan cheese

**1.** Twenty-four to 36 hours ahead, place the fish in a large pot with enough cold water to cover and refrigerate. Change the water every 8 hours. Prior to cooking, rinse one last time and drain. Bring a large pot of water to a rolling boil, add the fish, then reduce the heat to maintain a gentle boil. Cook for 10 to 15 minutes, until the fish is tender. Using a slotted spoon, transfer the fish to a bowl and set aside to cool. Keeping the water at a gentle boil, add the potatoes and cook for 10 to 15 minutes, until tender. Drain and set aside to cool.

**2.** Remove the skin and any bones from the cod, then flake, using your fingers or a fork. Peel the potatoes and mash them lightly. In the bowl of a food processor, combine the cod, potatoes, 2 tablespoons oil, and several turns of the pepper mill. Process several seconds to combine. Scrape down the sides of the processor, then process again, adding 2 more tablespoons oil down the feed tube while the machine is running. Continue to process until the mixture has the consistency of creamy mashed potatoes. Set aside.

**3.** In a large skillet, heat the remaining 3 tablespoons oil over medium heat. Add the peppers and the onion and sauté for 3 to 4 minutes, stirring frequently, until the vegetables begin to soften. Add the tomatoes, garlic, parsley, and the olives and stir to combine. Salt very lightly. Cook, stirring occasionally, for 15 minutes.

**4.** Preheat the oven to 425°F. Add the cod mixture to the vegetable mixture and stir gently with a wooden spoon to combine. Reduce the heat to medium-low and cook for 10 minutes. Remove from the heat and transfer the mixture to a buttered 10-inch round or 11-by-7-inch oval baking dish. Sprinkle the top evenly with the cheese and bake for 20 to 30 minutes, until the top is well browned. Serve immediately.

# Provençal Zucchini Gratin

SERVES 4 to 6

INGREDIENTS:

Fine sea salt

2 pounds zucchini, sliced into 1/4-inch rounds

3 tablespoons extra-virgin olive oil

1 pound tomatoes, peeled (plunged into boiling water for 30 seconds to facilitate peeling) and quartered

3 cloves garlic, finely chopped

1/3 cup finely chopped parsley

2 medium onions, chopped

6 anchovy fillets in olive oil, drained

2 large eggs

1/4 cup crème fraîche

2/3 cup milk

Freshly ground black pepper

12 fresh basil leaves, thinly julienned

1/2 cup grated Parmesan cheese

1. In a large pot of boiling salted water, blanch the zucchini for 1 minute. Drain and set aside.

2. In a large skillet, heat the oil over medium-high heat. Add the tomatoes and sauté, stirring frequently, until they begin to soften and give off their juice, about 4 minutes. Add the garlic, parsley, and onions and stir to combine. Cook for 5 minutes, stirring frequently, then add the anchovies and stir to combine. Cook for another minute and then remove from the heat and set aside.

3. Preheat to oven to 425°F. In a mixing bowl, combine the eggs, crème fraîche, milk, and a pinch of salt and pepper and beat to blend. Spread the zucchini over the bottom of a buttered 10 1/2-inch round or 11-by-7-inch oval baking dish. Spoon the tomato mixture over the zucchini, pour in the egg mixture, sprinkle with the basil and cheese, and bake for 20 to 30 minutes, until the topping is browned and bubbling. Serve immediately.

## Escarole and Caramelized Baby Onion Gratin

SERVES 4 to 6

INGREDIENTS:

Fine sea salt

2 pounds escarole, leaves washed well and separated

1 stick (8 table-spoons) unsalted butter

10 small fresh spring onions, or large pearl onions, peeled

2 tablespoons sugar

Coarsely ground black pepper

1/4 pound Yukon Gold potatoes, peeled and grated

1/4 pound slab bacon, rind removed, cut into 2-by-1/2-by-1/2-inch strips

1/3 cup finely chopped parsley

1/2 cup chicken stock

**1.** Bring a large pot of salted water to a rolling boil, add the escarole, and blanch for 4 minutes. Drain, then lay out the leaves on paper towels to dry. Set aside.

**2.** In a medium skillet, melt 3 tablespoons butter over medium heat. Add the onions, stir to coat, and sauté, stirring frequently, for 3 minutes. Sprinkle on the sugar, stir to coat, and cook, stirring frequently, until the onions caramelize to a golden brown, about 5 to 7 minutes. Season with pepper and set aside.

**3.** In a medium skillet, heat 3 tablespoons butter over medium-high heat. Add the potatoes and bacon and stir to combine. Cook, stirring frequently, for about 10 minutes, until the mixture is nicely browned. Set aside.

**4.** Loosely roll up the escarole leaves and arrange like the spokes of a wheel in a small buttered casserole about 10 inches in diameter. Spoon the potato mixture in between the leaves. Place the onions in the center of the casserole, like the hub of a wheel. Sprinkle with the parsley, pour in the chicken stock, cover, and cook over medium heat for 10 minutes. Reduce the heat to medium-low, and simmer for 20 minutes. Remove the cover and continue cooking until the liquid has evaporated, about 2 to 3 minutes.

**5.** Meanwhile, preheat the oven to 425°F. Bake the casserole in the center of the oven for 30 minutes. Serve immediately.

# Stuffed Tomato Gratin

SERVES 6

INGREDIENTS:

6 large ripe tomatoes

2 tablespoons unsalted butter

3/4 pound chopped sirloin

1 large egg

1/4 cup milk

Fine sea salt

Freshly ground black pepper

1/3 cup chopped Italian parsley

3 cloves garlic, minced

1 medium onion, minced

1/3 cup plus 2 tablespoons finely julienned fresh basil

1/3 cup unseasoned bread crumbs

2/3 cup grated Parmesan cheese

**1.** Cut a 1/2-inch slice, horizontally, off the stem end (top) of the tomatoes and set aside. Scoop out the pulp and set aside in a bowl. Grease a 10-inch round or 11-by-7-inch rectangular baking dish with the butter. Place the tomatoes in the dish and set aside.

**2.** In a mixing bowl, combine the sirloin, egg, and milk and stir to blend. Add generous pinches of salt and pepper and stir to combine. Add the parsley, garlic, onion, 1/3 cup basil, and the bread crumbs and stir to combine.

**3.** Preheat the oven to 425°F. Spoon the meat filling into the tomatoes, mounding it slightly at the top (the filling will expand as it cooks). Top the tomatoes with their caps. Spoon the reserved pulp around the tomatoes, then drizzle the oil over the pulp. Sprinkle with the cheese and the remaining 2 tablespoons basil. Bake in the center of the oven for 30 to 40 minutes, until the top of the stuffing is nicely browned. Serve immediately.

**Christophe's suggestion:** To help the tomatoes sit upright properly as they bake, you can scatter about 1/2 cup of plain white or sticky rice in the bottom of the baking dish. When you place the tomatoes in the baking dish shuffle them around slightly to find their ideal position.

# Celery Root and Thyme Gratin

SERVES 4 to 6

INGREDIENTS:

Fine sea salt

1 large celery root (about 1 pound) peeled, cut into 1/4-inch rounds, then into 2-by-1/2-inch strips

1 stick plus 1 table-spoon (9 table-spoons) unsalted butter

3 tablespoons flour

1/4 cup cold milk

Freshly ground black pepper

3/4 cup crème fraîche

2 sprigs thyme

1 cup grated Gruyère cheese

**1.** Bring a large pot of salted water to a boil, add the celery root, and cook for about 10 minutes, until just tender. Drain and set aside.

**2.** Meanwhile, in a large skillet, melt 7 tablespoons butter. Sprinkle in the flour, whisking constantly to blend, and cook for 1 minute. Add the milk, whisking constantly, then season to taste with salt and pepper. Add the crème fraîche and whisk to blend. Cook for another 2 to 3 minutes, until the mixture has thickened. Remove the sauce from the heat and set aside.

**3.** Preheat the oven to 450°F. With the remaining 2 tablespoons butter, grease a 10 1/2-inch round or 11-by-7-inch oval baking dish, then spread the celery root over the bottom. Pour the cream sauce over the celery root, lay the thyme on top, and sprinkle with the cheese. Bake in the center of the oven for about 15 minutes, until the topping is bubbling and nicely browned. Serve immediately.

# Gratin Parmentier: French Shepherd's Pie

SERVES 4 to 6

INGREDIENTS:

Fine sea salt

3 pounds medium baking potatoes, such as russetts, peeled and quartered

1 cup milk

5 tablespoons unsalted butter

Freshly ground black pepper

1 pound ground sirloin (or 1/2 pound each of sirloin and lamb)

1 large egg

3 cloves garlic, crushed

1/3 cup coarsely chopped parsley

2 shallots, finely chopped

1 cup unseasoned bread crumbs

3 tablespoons extra-virgin olive oil

1 cup grated Gruyère cheese

1. Bring a large pot of salted water to a boil, add the potatoes, and cook for 20 to 25 minutes, until the potatoes are just tender when pierced with the tip of a small sharp knife. Meanwhile, in a small saucepan or in a microwave oven, heat 1/2 cup milk until very hot but not boiling. Drain the potatoes, mash finely to the consistency of a puree (or press through a potato ricer), add the hot milk and 2 tablespoons butter, a generous pinch of salt, and several turns of the pepper mill, and stir until smoothly blended with no lumps. Set aside.

2. In a large mixing bowl, combine the sirloin, egg, garlic, parsley, and shallots and stir to combine. Add the remaining 1/2 cup milk, a generous pinch of salt, several turns of the pepper mill, and the bread crumbs and stir to incorporate.

3. In a large skillet, heat the oil over medium-high heat, then add the meat mixture and brown lightly, stirring frequently, until meat is just cooked through, about 10 minutes. Meanwhile, preheat the oven to 425°F.

4. With 1 1/2 tablespoons butter, grease the bottom and sides of a 10-inch round or 11-by-7-inch oval baking dish. Spread the meat mixture in the bottom of the dish, then top with the pureed potato mixture, covering the meat entirely and smoothing the surface. Scatter the cheese evenly over the potatoes. Chop the remaining 1 1/2 tablespoons butter and dot the bits over the top. Cook in the center of the oven for about 30 minutes, until the top is well browned and bubbling. Serve immediately.

# Oyster and Champagne Gratin

SERVES 2

INGREDIENTS:

6 large oysters on the half-shell, with their juice

4 tablespoons Champagne

3 large eggs

1/4 cup crème fraîche

1/2 cup grated Gruyère cheese

1. Remove the oysters from their shells and pour their juice through a fine strainer; set the shells aside on a large plate. In a medium nonstick skillet, combine the oyster juice, oysters, and Champagne, and bring to a boil over medium heat. Immediately remove from the heat and transfer the oysters back into their shells using a slotted spoon. Place the oyster shells on a baking sheet or in a baking dish and set aside.

2. Preheat the broiler. Return the skillet to medium heat and cook until the liquid is reduced by half. Meanwhile, in a small bowl, combine the eggs and the crème fraîche and beat to blend. Add the egg mixture to the skillet and cook, whisking constantly, until the mixture is thick, smooth, and airy. Remove from the heat. Spoon the sauce over the oysters, sprinkle with the cheese, and place under the broiler for about 3 minutes, until the sauce is lightly browned and bubbling. Serve immediately.

# Green Cabbage Gratin

SERVES 4 to 6

INGREDIENTS:

Fine sea salt

2 small heads green cabbage, quartered, cored, and thinly sliced crosswise

3 tablespoons extra-virgin olive oil

3 tomatoes, peeled (plunged into boiling water for 30 seconds to facilitate peeling) and seeded

1 medium onion, thinly sliced

3 cloves garlic, finely chopped

1/3 cup chopped Italian parsley

Freshly ground black pepper

1/2 cup freshly grated Parmesan cheese

**1.** Bring a large pot of salted water to a rolling boil, add the cabbage, and cook until just tender, about 4 to 5 minutes. Drain and set aside.

**2.** In a large skillet, heat the oil over medium heat. Add the tomatoes, onion, garlic, and parsley. Stir to combine. Raise the heat to high, then cook, stirring frequently, for 2 minutes. Add the cabbage and salt and pepper to taste and stir to combine. Cook, stirring frequently, for 10 minutes. Preheat the oven to 425°F.

**3.** Transfer the cabbage mixture to a buttered 10-inch round or 11-by-7-inch oval baking dish (or use 4 to 6 individual gratin dishes), sprinkle with the cheese, and bake for 15 to 20 minutes, until the top is browned and bubbling. Serve immediately.

# Asparagus and Pea Gratin

SERVES 4 to 6

INGREDIENTS:

| | | |
|---|---|---|
| 1 pound shelled fresh peas | 6 tablespoons unsalted butter | Freshly grated nutmeg |
| 1/2 pound slim asparagus, spears trimmed to 4 inches long | 3 tablespoons flour | Freshly ground black pepper |
| | 1 cup cold milk | 1 cup grated Gruyère cheese |
| | Fine sea salt | |

**1.** In separate pots of gently boiling salted water, cook the peas and the asparagus for 4 to 10 minutes, until just tender. Drain and set aside.

**2.** In a heavy-bottom saucepan, heat 4 tablespoons butter over medium heat. Sprinkle in the flour and whisk to blend, then gradually add the milk, whisking constantly. Add a pinch of salt, a pinch of nutmeg, and several turns of the pepper mill and stir to blend. Remove the sauce from the heat and set aside.

**3.** Preheat the broiler. With the remaining 2 tablespoons butter, grease a 10-inch round or 11-by-7-inch oval baking dish (you can also prepare this in 4 to 6 individual gratin dishes), mound the peas in the center, then arrange the asparagus around them. Pour the sauce over the vegetables, and sprinkle with the cheese and another pinch of nutmeg. Broil for 4 to 5 minutes, until the cheese topping is nicely browned. Serve immediately.

# Fresh Fig and Fennel Gratin

SERVES 4 to 6

INGREDIENTS:

10 large purple figs

1 3/4 cups red Banyuls wine (a sweet French dessert wine), or tawny port

3 bay leaves

1 sprig thyme

1 whole clove

Freshly ground black pepper

3 tablespoons extra-virgin olive oil

4 small fennel bulbs, branches trimmed, quartered

Fine sea salt

1/4 pound Parmesan cheese, finely shaved

**1.** Using the tines of a fork, prick the figs in several places, then combine in a mixing bowl with the wine, bay leaves, thyme, clove, and several turns of the pepper mill. Set aside to marinate for 3 to 4 hours at room temperature.

**2.** Strain the marinade into a medium saucepan, add the figs, and cook over medium-low heat for 35 minutes, stirring occasionally. Set the saucepan aside.

**3.** Meanwhile, in a medium skillet, heat the oil over medium heat. Add the fennel, stir to coat, and sauté for about 10 minutes, stirring frequently, until lightly browned and just tender. Season to taste with salt and pepper, remove from the heat, and set aside.

**4.** Preheat the oven to 350°F. Butter a 10 1/2-inch round or 11-by-7-inch baking dish and, using a slotted spoon, lift the figs from the marinade and place them in the dish. Scatter on the fennel, then spoon 7 tablespoons of the marinade over the fennel. Bake in the center of the oven for 20 minutes. Open the oven door and sprinkle the cheese over the mixture and cook for another 20 minutes, until the cheese is browned and bubbling. Serve immediately.

**Christophe's suggestion:** This gratin is a particularly tasty accompaniment to a roast duck, goose, or capon.

# Pumpkin and Chorizo Gratin

SERVES 4 to 6

INGREDIENTS:

Fine sea salt

1 small pumpkin (about 3 pounds), quartered, peeled, seeded, strings removed, then cut into bite-sized chunks

Freshly ground black pepper

5 tablespoons unsalted butter

1 clove garlic, lightly crushed

3 medium onions, thinly sliced

1/4 pound chorizo sausage, thinly sliced

1 1/4 cup grated Gruyère cheese

3 tablespoons extra-virgin olive oil

**1.** Bring a large pot of salted water to a boil, add the pumpkin, and cook until just tender, about 10 minutes. Drain, season with a pinch of salt and pepper, and set aside.

**2.** Preheat the oven to 425°F. With 2 tablespoons butter, coat a 10 1/2-inch round or 11-by-7-inch oval baking dish. Rub the bottom and the sides of the dish with the garlic. Spread half of the pumpkin over the bottom of the dish. Cover the pumpkin layer with half of the onions and then cover the onions with half of the chorizo. Repeat this process with the remaining pumpkin, onion, and chorizo, then season to taste with salt and pepper. Chop the remaining 3 tablespoons butter into little bits and scatter over the top, then sprinkle with the cheese. Drizzle the oil evenly over the top and bake in the center of the oven for 20 to 30 minutes, until the topping is browned and bubbling. Serve immediately.

# Eggplant Parmesan Gratin

SERVES 4 to 6

INGREDIENTS:

5 tablespoons extra-virgin olive oil

5 medium eggplants, cut into 1/2-inch slices, then into 1 1/2-by-1 1/2-inch strips

Fine sea salt

Coarsley ground black pepper

1 1/4 cup grated Parmesan cheese

**1.** In a large nonreactive skillet, warm the oil over medium-high heat. Add the eggplant and generous pinches of salt and pepper and stir to combine. Reduce the heat to medium and cook, stirring frequently, for about 10 minutes, until the eggplant is tender. Remove from the heat and set aside.

**2.** Meanwhile, preheat the oven to 425°F. In a buttered 10 1/2-inch round or 11-by-7-inch oval baking dish (or 4 to 6 individual gratin dishes), spread the eggplant over the bottom, then sprinkle evenly with the cheese. Bake in the center of the oven for 20 to 30 minutes, until the cheese topping is nicely browned. Serve immediately.

# Swiss Chard and Roquefort Cheese Gratin

SERVES 4 to 6

INGREDIENTS:

Fine sea salt

2 pounds Swiss chard, stems cut into 1/2-inch pieces, leaves halved lengthwise

2 tablespoons extra-virgin olive oil

Freshly ground black pepper

2 large eggs

1/4 cup crème fraîche

4 tablespoons unsalted butter

1 cup crumbled Roquefort cheese

7 long chives, cut into 1/2-inch pieces

**1.** Bring a large pot of salted water to a boil. Add the Swiss chard stems and cook for 2 minutes, then add the Swiss chard leaves and cook for another 4 minutes. Drain and set aside.

**2.** In a skillet, heat the oil over medium heat. Add the Swiss chard and generous pinches of salt and pepper and stir to coat the leaves. Cook for 1 minute. Remove from the heat and set aside.

**3.** Preheat the oven to 425°F. In a small bowl, combine the eggs and the crème fraîche and beat to blend. Set aside.

**4.** Coat a 10 1/2-inch round or 11-by-7-inch oval baking dish with 2 tablespoons butter. Spread the Swiss chard over the bottom, pour in the egg mixture, then sprinkle on the cheese and all but 1 tablespoon of the chives. Cut the remaining 2 tablespoons butter into bits and scatter over the top. Bake in the center of the oven for about 20 minutes, until the top is nicely browned. Garnish with the remaining of chives and serve immediately.

**Mango**
Banana, Mango, and Currant Gratin  44
Tropical Fruit Gratin with Malibu Sabayon  62

**Mirabelle Plum**
Semolina and Mirabelle Gratin  34
Chocolate, Mirabelle, and Thyme Gratin  64

**Orange**
Earl Grey Tea-Marinated Prunes with Sabayon Gratin  27
Semolina and Mirabelle Gratin  34
Orange, Dark Chocolate, and Litchi Gratin  42
Pear and Poached-Peach Gratin with Crème de Cassis  49
Banana-Orange Gratin with Caramelized Pecans  74
Gratin of Honeyed Citrus with Crumbled Meringue  77

**Papaya**
Papaya, Pineapple, and Peppered Lemon Gratin with
    Orange Sabayon  30
Tropical Fruit Gratin with Malibu Sabayon  62

**Passion Fruit**
Raspberry-Passion Fruit Gratin in Puff Pastry  11

**Peach**
Pear and Poached-Peach Gratin with Crème de Cassis  49
White Peach and Currant Gratin with Coconut Sorbet  50
Peach and Almond Cream Gratin with Strawberry
    Rosemary Sauce  52
White Peach and Apricot Gratin with Hazelnut
    Sabayon  58

**Peanut**
Almond, Apricot, and Peanut Gratin  22

**Pear**
Chestnut Cream and Pear Gratin  17
Sour Cherry, Pear, and Pistachio Gratin  45
Pear and Poached-Peach Gratin with Crème de Cassis  49
Grapefruit and Pear Gratin with Pistachio Sabayon  60
Pear Soufflé Gratin with Saffron and Chocolate  61

**Pineapple**
Papaya, Pineapple, and Peppered Lemon Gratin with
    Orange Sabayon  30
Pineapple Gratin à la Piña Colada  39
Tropical Fruit Gratin with Malibu Sabayon  62
Pineapple and Mixed-Cherry with Kirsch Gratin  69

**Pecan**
Banana-Orange Gratin with Caramelized Pecans  74

**Pistachio**
Earl Grey Tea-Marinated Prunes with Sabayon Gratin  27
Sautéed Apricot with Walnut Gratin and Port
    Sabayon  28
Sour Cherry, Pear, and Pistachio Gratin  45
Grapefruit and Pear Gratin with Pistachio Sabayon  60

**Prune**
Earl Grey Tea-Marinated Prunes with Sabayon Gratin  27
Sour Cherry, Pear, and Pistachio Gratin  45

**Raspberry**
Raspberry-Passion Fruit Gratin in Puff Pastry  11
Red Berry Gratin with Pink Champagne Sabayon  36
Fromage Blanc Gratin with Assorted Red Berries  53
Red and Black Berry Gratin with Lemon-Zest
    Meringue  57
Fig with Cinnamon and Fresh Almond Gratin  65
Raspberry Gratin with Cola Sabayon  70

**Rhubarb**
Vanilla Rhubarb Gratin  31
Banana, Strawberry, and Rhubarb Gratin  82

**Sour Cherry**
Sour Cherry, Pear, and Pistachio Gratin  45

**Strawberry**
Red Berry Gratin with Pink Champagne Sabayon  36
Peach and Almond Cream Gratin with Strawberry-
    Rosemary Sauce  52
Fromage Blanc Gratin with Assorted Red Berries  53
Wild Strawberry and Olive Oil Gratin with Lemon
    Sabayon  71
Gratin of Wild Strawberries and Creamy Lime
    Meringue  76
Summer Fruit Gratin  80
Banana, Strawberry, and Rhubarb Gratin  82

**Walnut**
Earl Grey Tea-Marinated Prunes with Sabayon
    Gratin  27
Sautéed Apricot and Walnut Gratin with Port
    Sabayon  28

**Pea**
Asparagus and Pea Gratin  146

**Pepper**
Ratatouille Gratin with Bay Leaves  94
Salt Cod Gratin Provençal  131

**Potato**
Potato and Muenster Gratin  92
Potato Gratin Dauphinois  106
Two-Salmon Gratin with Potatoes and Chives  109
Cucumber and Pancetta Gratin  125
Salt Cod Gratin Provençal  131
Gratin Parmentier: French Shepherd's Pie  141

**Prawn**
Saffron-Spiced Shellfish Gratin  120

**Prosciutto**
Endive and Prosciutto Gratin  96

**Pumpkin**
Pumpkin and Chorizo Gratin  149

**Roquefort Cheese**
Swiss Chard and Roquefort Cheese Gratin  153

**Salmon**
Two-Salmon Gratin with Potatoes and Chives  109

**Salsify**
Chicken Liver and Salsify Gratin  95

**Sausage**
Pumpkin and Chorizo Gratin  149

**Sea Scallop**
Sea Scallop Gratin  113
Saffron-Spiced Shellfish Gratin  120
Baked Seafood Gratin  122

**Shrimp**
Saffron-Spiced Shellfish Gratin  120
Baked Seafood Gratin  122

**Spinach**
Spinach Gratin with Raclette Cheese  87

**Snail**
Escargot à la Française Gratin  100

**Swiss Chard**
Swiss Chard and Roquefort Cheese Gratin  153

**Tomato**
Leek and Tomato Gratin with Basil  90
Ratatouille Gratin with Bay Leaves  94
Gratin of Garden Vegetables  101
Baby Shell Pasta with Tomato and Egg Gratin  104
Haddock and Tomato Gratin  130
Salt Cod Gratin Provençal  131
Provençal Zucchini Gratin  134
Stuffed Tomato Gratin  137
Green Cabbage Gratin  143

**Tuna**
Macaroni and Tuna Gratin  98

**Turnip**
Gratin of Garden Vegetables  101

**Zucchini**
Ratatouille Gratin with Bay Leaves  94
Gratin of Garden Vegetables  101
Stuffed Zucchini Gratin  124
Provençal Zucchini Gratin  134

# Acknowledgments

We would like to thank,
Baccarat, Les Toiles du Soleil, Raynaud, Ercruis,
Cristal de Sèvres, Kitchen Bazaar, Jean-Louis Coquet, Scof, R. Haviland and
C. Parlon, Yves Déshoulières, Olaria, Tharaud, Geneviève Lethu, Le Jacquard Français,
Garnier Thiébaut, Alexandre Turpault, La Carpe, Le Cèdre Rouge,
Déco du Monde, and Du Bout du Monde.

*—Lisbeth Kwik*

Text copyright © 2001 Christophe Felder
Translation by Linda Dannenberg
Photographs copyright © 2001 Jean-Louis Motte
Stylist: Lisbeth Kwik

All rights reserved. No portion of this book may be reproduced,
stored in a retrieval system, or transmitted in any form or by any means,
mechanical, electronic, photocopying, recording, or otherwise,
without written permission from the publisher.

Published by
Éditions Minerva
A Company of La Martinière Groupe
2, rue Christine
75006 Paris, France

U.S. Distribution:
Harry N. Abrams, Inc.
A Company of La Martinière Groupe
100 Fifth Avenue
New York, NY 10011

Canadian Distribution:
Canadian Manda Group
One Atlantic Avenue, Suite 105
Toronto, Ontario M6K 3E7, Canada

Library of Congress
Cataloging-in-Publication Data
Felder, Christophe.
[Gratins de Christophe. English]
Gratins : golden-crusted sweet and savory dishes /
Christophe Felder ;
translator Linda Dannenberg ;
photographer Jean-Louis Motte ;
stylist Lisbeth Kwik.
p. cm.
ISBN 1-58479-257-4
I. Cookery, French.
I. Title.
TX 719+    2002068999

Printed in Italy by Vincenzo Bona
Text set in Scala and Scala Sans.
10 9 8 7 6 5 4 3 2 1
*First Printing 2002*